Implementing
a Training and
Develo
Strateg

Roger Cartwright

T0209197

- Fast-track route to making your training and development strategy an integral part of the overall goals and strategies of your organization

- Covers how to make training and development an effective cyclical process, which encompasses identification, planning, implementation and evaluation leading back to redefined training needs. Also ensures that organizational goals match individual aspiration

- Case studies of the corporate arm of the Open University, Kentucky Fried Chicken/Yum Brands, Kodak, The Famous Grouse Experience, Hong Kong Mass Transit

- Includes a comprehensive resources guide, key concepts and thinkers, a 10-step action plan and a section of FAQs

TRAINING & DEVELOPMENT

11.08

First Published 2003 by
Capstone Publishing Limited (a Wiley company)
8 Newtec Place
Magdalen Road
Oxford OX4 1RE
United Kingdom
http://www.capstoneideas.com

CIP catalogue records for this book are available from the British Library and the US Library of Congress

ISBN 1-84112-449-4

Wiley also publishes its books in a variety of electronic formats. Some content that appears in print may not be available in electronic books.

Websites often change their contents and addresses; details of sites listed in this book were accurate at the time of writing, but may change.

Contents

Introduction to ExpressExec

ExpressExec is a completely up-to-date resource of current business practice, accessible in a number of ways – anytime, anyplace,
anywhere. ExpressExec combines best practice cases, key ideas, action
points, glossaries, further reading, and resources.

Each module contains 10 individual titles that cover all the key
aspects of global business practice. Written by leading experts in their
field, the knowledge imparted provides executives with the tools and
skills to increase their personal and business effectiveness, benefiting
both employee and employer.

ExpressExec is available in a number of formats:

» **Print** – 120 titles available through retailers or printed on demand
  using any combination of the 1200 chapters available.
» **E-Books** – e-books can be individually downloaded from Express-
  Exec.com or online retailers onto PCs, handheld computers, and
  e-readers.
» **Online** – http://www.expressexec.wiley.com/ provides fully search-
  able access to the complete ExpressExec resource via the Internet – a
  cost-effective online tool to increase business expertise across a
  whole organization.

» **ExpressExec Performance Support Solution (EEPSS)** – a software solution that integrates ExpressExec content with interactive tools to provide organizations with a complete internal management development solution.

» **ExpressExec Rights and Syndication** – ExpressExec content can be licensed for translation or display within intranets or on Internet sites.

To find out more visit www.ExpressExec.com or contact elound@wiley-capstone.co.uk.

Introduction to Implementing a Training and Development Strategy

This chapter considers:

- » training and development as an investment in the human resource;
- » training and development as a partnership between the organization and the individual;
- » the need for training and development to be evaluated;
- » the importance of value for money from training and development activities; and
- » the increasing importance of lifelong learning.

Andrew Mayo (1998) has noted that the mid-1990s were a time when organizations began to realize that their human/intellectual capital was as important as – if not more important than – all their physical and financial assets.

Organizational growth, change and success ultimately depend on the actions of human beings. Training and development are the ways in which an organization invests in its human capital. Like all investments, the aim is that the organization should receive a benefit from its investment. Benefits are reflected in what has become known as the bottom line. The bottom line is not just measured by raw profit figures but by the relative profits and market share of the organization measured against the organization's competitors.

Training and development do not come cheap, but in a competitive commercial environment a failure to realize the human potential within an organization can be very costly. Training and development are not only the responsibility of the organization, but also of the individual employees.

Given that training and development require an investment by both the individual and the organization, an investment that can be measured in both financial and time terms, it is important that both partners receive value for money.

Training and development do not occur in an organizational vacuum – they should be linked to the overall goals and strategies of the organization and to the life goals and strategies of the individual.

This material is designed to assist organizations in considering how training and development can be progressed in line with the needs of both the organization and the individual, implemented in the most effective way and, of critical importance, evaluated to ensure that the training and development have achieved the intended result.

As will be considered in the next chapter, training and development are different activities. Training is concerned with skills, whilst development includes not only skills but also attitudes and attributes. Training tends to be short term whilst development is an activity that can last for an entire career and beyond. The concept of lifelong learning is one that has grown in importance. Lifelong learning carries with it the premise that nobody is too old to learn new skills. As the idea of a "job for life" has disappeared throughout much of the commercial world, the changes in career that more and more individuals are having to accept carry with them a need for continuous training and development.

The idea that training and development along with education are activities concentrated at the beginning of a working life is one that is long past its sell-by date. Successful organizations – as will be shown in the case studies in this material – recognize the importance of investing in training and development and successful individuals realize that learning is a continuous process. Successful individuals also recognize that they need to invest in themselves in order to make themselves as attractive as possible in the employment stakes.

What is Meant by a Training and Development Strategy?

This chapter examines the following concepts relating to training and development strategies:

» training and development linked to the overall goals and strategies of an organization;
» the responsibilities of the individual;
» human capital as an intangible asset;
» learning as a permanent change in behavior;
» training to gain and improve skills;
» development as a long-term process that not only provides skills but changes attitudes;
» education as a social process that transmits societal norms to individuals;
» individual attention through coaching and mentoring;
» the strategic training and development cycle; and
» training and development – role in recruitment and retention.

INTANGIBLE ASSETS

Organizations typically measure their assets in tangible terms – stock, buildings, investments, cash etc.

However, in addition to these there are intangible assets that may have a value far in excess of the more tangible assets. Trademarks, brand names and patents are examples of intangible assets. One of the most important intangible assets that an organization possesses is that of human capital – the value of the experience, loyalty, knowledge, and attributes of the employees.

DEFINITIONS

Within any study of training and development there is a series of definitions that need to be introduced. These definitions are covered in detail in *Training and Development Express* (2003), companion material in the ExpressExec series. The most important definitions are those for:

» learning
» training
» development
» education
» coaching
» mentoring.

Each of the above should be part of the training and development strategy of the organization.

LEARNING

Learning is the process by which behavior and attitudes are changed. One of the major debates in child development and education has been on the question of how much behavior is innate and how much is learnt – the "nature or nurture" debate.

A psychological definition of learning is "any change in the general activity of an organism the effects of which persist and recur over a period of time and which are strengthened by repetition and practice" (Thomson, 1959). Although this is quite an old definition, it covers the major points about learning very comprehensively – the fact that learning persists and recurs and that it is strengthened by repetition and practice. Indeed, if the new behavior does not persist then it is generally accepted that learning has not occurred.

TRAINING

Training is very specific and is concerned with the mastering of a particular task or set of tasks.

At its most basic, training does not require understanding of the whys and wherefores. It is fairly easy to train a pigeon to select a particular shape from a collection of shapes or a Seeing Eye dog to guide a human being around obstacles or to sniff out drugs and explosives. The training process with animals involves rewards and punishments – a food treat as reward and a harsh word etc. as a punishment. The pigeon and the dog can perform very competently but there is no evidence to suggest that they know why they are behaving in this way, only that at some time in the past this type of behavior gained the animal a reward. With humans, training that encompasses a degree of "why?" tends to be more effective than training that does not. However, one can train an individual to use a computer for word processing without the individual understanding very much about how microprocessors actually work. Effective training provides the right degree of knowledge to underpin the task.

In the case of work-based training and development, punishment should never be used as this will cause the trainee to associate training with something unpleasant (punishment). Training and development may be challenging, but it should not be so unpleasant as to put the trainee off the subject. The ability to judge the degree to which the trainee should be challenged without becoming distressed is something that trainers gain with experience. Trainees should always be able to experience an adequate degree of success, as success is a motivator, whilst too much failure is a demotivator.

A distinction needs to be made between imposed punishments and rewards and the way individuals might "kick themselves" when they make a mistake or feel proud when all goes well.

The effectiveness of training is measured by examining what a person could do before the training and what they can do after it. The difference may be in being actually able to perform a new task or an improvement in the manner of carrying out an old task.

DEVELOPMENT

Development is a process in which learning occurs through experience and where the results of the learning enhance not only the task skills of the individual but also his or her attitudes. Whereas training does not necessarily encompass the why, development most certainly does. Development provides the individual with skills and attributes that can be changed to fit new circumstances.

Whereas training can be measured objectively – before the training the person could not do X, after the training they can do X – development is much more subjective. Development not only provides skills, but also changes the way the individual thinks and reasons. Training is mechanical; development is humanistic (Lessem, 1990). Training may be accomplished in a relatively short time frame – development, linked as it is to intellectual growth, takes much longer. The importance of organizationally based development is that the individual's development can occur in an environment where the development processes and activities can be linked to the culture and aims of the organization.

EDUCATION

Used in its formal sense, education is the broadening of the knowledge and skills base of the individual and indeed the group with the objective of the individual functioning in and being a benefit to the society he or she lives in.

Development, as discussed earlier, is a process in which learning occurs through experience and where the results of the learning enhance not only the task skills of the individual but also his or her attitudes. Education is where individuals learn about the norms operating in their society. Education is an investment by a society into its members with the ultimate aim of benefiting that society.

Formal education is usually provided by or in conjunction with those who are in charge of a particular society.

COACHING

Like training, coaching is concerned with skills, whether they are sporting skills or work skills. Every top-class athlete has a coach who works with him or her to improve technique. Coaching has always been an important component of apprenticeship schemes. Coaching has seen a resurgence in recent years as organizations realize that it is an ideal method of transferring the skills and knowledge of older and more experienced employees to new hires. It also helps ensure that the intellectual capital of the organization is not diminished when an employee retires or leaves, as the skills and knowledge will have been passed on through the coaching process.

MENTORING

What coaching is to training, mentoring is to development. A mentor is not concerned solely with improving skills and performance in a narrow range of tasks but with the development of the whole individual. A mentor is an experienced person other than the individual's manager who provides counsel and guidance to assist the individual in his or her organizational growth.

It is important that the mentor does not have a line management relationship with the individual, as that could cause a conflict of interest.

Training and development is the means by which an organization invests in its employees. Change requires new skills and attitudes and thus organizations that do not invest in training and development cannot hope to benefit from change – indeed they may well not survive change.

TRAINING AND DEVELOPMENT STRATEGY AS PART OF THE OVERALL STRATEGY OF THE ORGANIZATION

Gerry Johnson and Kevan Scholes (1984) define strategy as "the direction and scope of an organization over the long term: ideally which matches its resources to its changing environment, and in particular its markets, customers or clients so as to meet stakeholder expectations."

Using the Johnson and Scholes definition applied to training and development, we can say that a training and development strategy is:

> the direction and scope of the training and development opportunities developed and provided by the organization for its employees and other concerned partners: ideally which matches the training and development provided to both the needs of the organization and the individual in order to ensure that the organization can respond to changes in its external environment.

The training and development strategy should form part of the overall strategy of the organization – it is nested within the overall strategy. Whilst this might seem common sense, there have cases where the training and development provided have not been linked to the overall strategy. Training has been provided, often at considerable cost but with little connection to what the organization needs. In the 1970s and 1980s many of the courses provided by the local school authorities in the UK for their teachers could be accessed not on a "needs of the school" basis but on the whim of a teacher. In many cases the principal (head teacher) did not have to approve attendance.

Changes in products and services nearly always carry with them a need for some training. If the organization does not have an effective training and development policy it may be less successful than its competitors when it comes to grasping new opportunities.

TRAINING AND DEVELOPMENT STRATEGIES

A training and development strategy comprises a number of components, all of which can be phrased as questions.

» What skills have our people at the moment?
» What are the future aims and direction of the organization?
» What skills will our people need to achieve the corporate aims?

The above form the basis for the overall strategy and a training needs analysis (TNA).

» From the TNA what training and development should be planned?
» Who will deliver the training and development?

» Who in the organization will receive the training and development?
» Are there stakeholders outside the organization who should receive training and development?

These components form the planning stage.

» How is the training and development to be implemented?

This is the implementation stage.

» How will the success of the training and development be monitored and evaluated?

This is the evaluation stage, which is likely to reveal new training needs.

The process is cyclical not linear. The cycle can be represented as shown in Fig. 2.1.

THE ROLE OF TRAINING AND DEVELOPMENT IN RECRUITMENT AND RETENTION

Organizations wish to recruit the most talented individuals possible and, provided that they show signs of fulfilling their potential, retain them in order to recoup the investment in the individual that the organization has made.

All organizations need to train staff at some time or other whether this is carried out in-house or by an external provider. Not all organizations see the need or are prepared to spend money on developing staff. Providing development opportunities gives recognition to the individual and recognition, as Herzberg (1962) showed, is one of the most powerful motivators there is. Development does not just provide new skills and ways of thinking – it can also motivate the individual.

The training and development strategy of an organization inputs into the organization's recruitment and retention policies in two ways.

First, there is little point in recruiting an individual with potential but who lacks the particular skills for the job if there are no procedures in place to provide training. It is unlikely that every potential employee will have all the skills that are required for the job and thus it is important that recruitment policies are supported by training.

Secondly, more and more talented individuals are seeking to work for organizations that have good training and development policies.

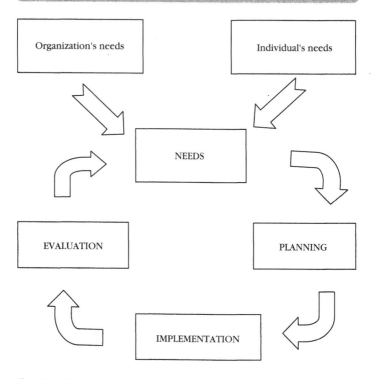

Fig. 2.1 The strategic training and development cycle.

Providing a development opportunity for an individual may make the difference as to whether the individual stays or goes.

KEY LEARNING POINTS
» Training and development is the means by which an organization invests in its employees.
» In addition to the tangible assets such as buildings and cash, organizations also possess intangible assets such as human capital.

» Learning is the process by which behavior and attitudes are changed.
» Training is very specific and is concerned with the mastering of a particular task or set of tasks.
» Development is a process in which learning occurs through experience and where the results of the learning enhance not only the task skills of the individual but also his or her attitudes.
» Training can be measured objectively, whilst the measurement of development is much more subjective.
» Coaching is the process of transferring the skills and knowledge of older and more experienced employees to the less experienced through a close relationship, usually face-to-face.
» A mentor is an experienced person other than the individual's manager who provides counsel and guidance to assist the individual in his or her organizational growth.
» Strategy is concerned with the overall direction of the organization.
» Development can be a powerful motivator.
» There is a link between the training and development strategy and the organization's recruitment and retention policies.
» The training and development strategy should be nested within the overall organizational strategy.
» The training and development process is cyclical, not linear.

The Evolution of Training and Development Strategies

This chapter considers how training and development has evolved. It explains:

» how the apprenticeship system was developed;
» the need for technical education and training brought about by the Industrial Revolution;
» the current need for work-based training and development;
» Continuous Professional Development (CPD); and
» partnerships between employers and the formal providers of education.

In many respects the story of training and development is as old as the human race itself. Details on the history of training and development can be found in the companion volume *Training and Development Express* (2003). This material concentrates on the linking of training and development strategies to overall organizational strategies since the Industrial Revolution.

WORKPLACE TRAINING AND DEVELOPMENT

Universal education is a fairly recent phenomenon and there are still many parts of the world where even a basic formal education is unavailable to most people.

However, the importance and need for work-based training in order to pass on skills and knowledge has been recognized since the earliest times for which we have records. Work-based training and development predates universal education. The idea of training the young for work tasks and using older members of the family, group, or tribe to pass on wisdom and expertise is a feature of higher primates and not just humans.

From the fourteenth century onwards in Europe, the apprenticeship system of learning the skills of a craft or trade from experts in the field by working with them for a set period of time became an important means by which skills were passed down. Such training was provided by the employer and formed the first formalized training and development.

The apprenticeship system was used extensively by the craft guilds in the Middle Ages. The word "guild" is derived from the German *Gilde* or *Hansa*, words referring to caravans of merchant traders. The Middle Ages saw the rise of craft guilds, which included in their membership all those engaged in any particular craft, and which monopolized the making and selling of a particular product within the cities in which they were organized.

The members of a craft guild were divided into three classes: masters, journeymen and apprentices. The master owned the raw material and the tools and sold the goods manufactured in his own shop for profit. The journeymen and apprentices lived in the master's house. The apprentices, who were beginners in the trade and learned it under the direction of the master, usually received only their board in return for the work they did. In many cases the apprentice was indentured to the master, the apprentice's parents paying the master a sum of money. During the time span of the indenture the apprentice received no wages and was legally bound to the master, who would train the apprentice in the particular trade. After an apprentice had completed his training he became a journeyman and was paid a fixed wage for his labor. In time, a journeyman might become a master.

The importance of the apprenticeship system to this material lies in the fact that the master invariably linked the training of apprentices to the needs of the business – the training strategy was an integral part of the overall strategy. Such terms were probably not used but there is no doubt that these were times that were just as commercially competitive as today. In a competitive environment value for money and a return on investment become even more important, hence the need for the apprentice to be able to assist in moving the business forward by learning new skills.

THE INDUSTRIAL REVOLUTION

The Industrial Revolution during the nineteenth century was a time of considerable technological progress and migration of labor facilitated by the steamship and the railways – themselves products of the Industrial Revolution. The concept of a seven-year indenture became impossible to sustain especially as changes in the legal status of individuals made binding a person to the same master difficult to enforce.

The new mechanical and engineering trades needed a means of training workers, especially those who migrated into them from agricultural work. A distinct differentiation between skilled and unskilled workers was a feature of the factories that sprang up throughout Europe and North America. The new (for the time) technologies of steam and later electricity required a trained workforce. It was no use a manufacturer having a strategy that involved the use of these technologies unless there was an available workforce trained in them.

Whilst the lowliest workers received just enough training to carry out their tasks efficiently there was also a need for skilled engineers and designers. A revised style of apprenticeships were seen as a highly beneficial method of providing a skilled workforce in those trades that demanded skill, and of retaining the knowledge and experience of older workers. The need to retain skills within an organization is just as important today as it was then, and skill retention should also form part of the overall organizational strategy.

No longer was the apprentice tied to a master although his (and very occasionally her) parents might have to pay a sum to the owner of the enterprise. The apprentice would be paired with an experienced worker who would train and teach on the job. Apprenticeships up until quite recently tended to be male dominated, but women entering factory work or domestic service would often be partnered with an older lady on a more informal basis.

THE CURRENT NEED FOR WORK-BASED TRAINING AND DEVELOPMENT

Formal education systems in nearly every part of the world are aimed at the younger members of society. The education system is designed to provide the basic skills of mathematics, reading, science, and the arts as well as passing on the cultural norms and values of the particular society. What the system cannot provide is the specific skills required for particular jobs. Provision in this area is best accomplished through specific programs geared to the job and the employer.

This does not mean that there is no link between formal education and training and development. The more formal an education a person has received, the more honed will be his or her basic skills and ability to reason and analyze. A person with a good basic education is likely to be more accomplished at learning new skills than somebody who lacks the basics. There are exceptions – George Eastman, the founder of Kodak (see Chapter 7), left school at 14. However, it should be noted that he had received teaching in basic numeracy and literacy and was proficient in both. The remainder of this material is concerned with training and development that is work-related, but the importance of a good grounding in basic skills should never be underemphasized.

The events of the Second World War and the increasing technological aspect to industry that the war demonstrated showed that a more educated population was no longer a luxury but a necessity. Social pressures and changes throughout the world also demanded that all citizens be granted access to universal education regardless of age, gender, or social position. Organizations and society have begun to work more closely together to ensure that the skills of school leavers are those that organizations require. However, it is still the case that many employers berate education systems for not producing school leavers with the basic skills that employers can then build upon through training and development.

The pace of technological change is such that it is becoming clear that the task of formal education is to produce minds that are inquiring, flexible, creative, and with the basics of numeracy and literacy and for organizations to provide the necessary work-related training and development that change requires.

VOCATIONAL TRAINING

What a formal education system could not accomplish was the training of engineers, mechanics and draftsmen (still a totally male-oriented profession in the nineteenth and early twentieth centuries). Even if the resources had been available, the pace of change was so rapid that the formal education system could not keep up.

Employers who needed the skills but lacked the resources to provide the necessary training in all but the most work-related tasks and were reluctant to allow staff time off for training were nevertheless prepared to help fund the development of vocational training institutes, often called Mechanics' Institutes.

Those employees who wished to further their careers were encouraged to attend such institutes in their own time, usually in the evening. From the 1880s onwards such vocational institutes were established in towns and cities the length and breadth of North America and Europe.

Whilst Mechanics' Institutes could provide a rudimentary technical training, they could not provide the broad scientific and technical foundations that were beginning to be needed for a wider range of occupations. Various types of technical colleges and institutes were developed in both North America and Europe to provide further and higher education that concentrated on the practical applications of science and technology. Caltech and MIT in the US and UMIST (University of Manchester Institute of Science and Technology) in the UK are amongst the best known in the world.

In 1969, in an effort to assist those who had not received the opportunity for higher education, the UK government founded the

Open University (OU) using television and radio in addition to printed material as the medium for study.

Since then the OU has provided higher education opportunities for 2 million students ranging from the ages of 17 to 94, as well as serving as a model for similar enterprises overseas.

IN-HOUSE PROGRAMS

The alternative to having employees taking time off work for training and study or having to use their leisure time is for the organization to facilitate the training itself. The latter years of the twentieth century saw a huge proliferation in both organization-based programs and companies offering training and development outside the formal education system that offered to design and implement such training courses for organizations. By providing in-house provision either resourced internally or externally, the organization can ensure that training meets the needs of the organization. As systems and procedures change, training needs are identified and met in a manner that is contextualized to the particular organization. In this way the training and development strategy can be closely aligned to the organization's overall strategy.

Small companies may well not have the resources to undertake their own training and development, but this does not mean that they should not have a training and development strategy. External providers can be used for generic skills training with the contextualization being accomplished using in-house coaches and mentors.

CONTINUOUS PROFESSIONAL DEVELOPMENT (CPD)

In a large number of careers and professions, the information and skills learnt upon entry rapidly become out of date. As the pace of technological change has increased, so the lifespan of a particular piece of knowledge has lessened. This has generated a need for Continuous Professional Development (CPD), a process that recognizes that there are lifelong learning and training needs. Many professions and employers now require members and employees to undertake regular CPD to ensure that their knowledge and skills are as up to date as possible. CPD is one of the most important developments in training and development today together with a growing appreciation that the learning methodologies used in school, college, and university are far from ideal when dealing with employees who have a wealth of experience. From the 1970s onwards it began to become apparent that adults learn in very different ways to children and that work-based training and development could not use the same techniques as schools.

For those organizations using professionals (and the vast majority do have some professional staff – accountants, personnel managers etc.) the CPD needs of the individual also need to become part of the organization's training and development strategy. The standards and requirements are often laid down by professional bodies rather then the employing organization.

PARTNERSHIPS

The whole training and development process from the identification of training needs through implementation and finally evaluation requires people with a distinct set of training and development skills.

As change becomes ever faster and as the need for CPD (see above) encompasses more and more professionals, it may be difficult for the organization to deliver all of its training and development strategy from its own resources.

Many of the European universities in their early days shunned contact with business and commerce. Academics sat in their "ivory towers" and taught whilst business and commerce were left to the ordinary people. It is of little wonder that there was a clear distinction and in many cases hostility between "town and gown." Oxford and Cambridge Universities in the UK had their own legal system until relatively recently whereby students (or academics) were tried by the university authorities for wrongdoing even if it was committed in the town.

US universities, almost from their inception, have had a much closer relationship with business and commerce. In the UK and much of Europe it was only after the First World War that universities and external organizations began to develop close relationships. The polytechnics were first into the field and began to offer what were known as "sandwich" courses, whereby a student spent part of his or her course at the college/university and part working on the shop floor or laboratory. Even in practical subjects such as teacher training, the formal institutions were heavily balanced towards theory rather than practice. In the late 1960s, when the writer was training as a teacher, he spent a mere nine weeks in total working in a classroom with children in a three-year course!

Universities and colleges have seen the advantage in closer relationships with external organizations. Such relationships allow the universities not only to provide valuable outside experience for their students, but also a development opportunity for academics who can use an industrial partnership to make their teaching more relevant to the needs of the outside world.

Organizations can benefit from the development opportunities that a development program devised in conjunction with an academic institution can provide for their staff. Such a program often provides an opportunity for the employee to step back from the day-to-day demands of his or her job and consider the wider environment that his or her organization is working in.

Major research projects now often include both organization and university staff working together. The benefit to organizations is evident by the large number of academic "chairs" endowed by major corporations and the boom in scientific research institutes that are university-owned but run on commercial lines.

Partnerships between organizations and academia also provide an opportunity for the organization to gain the benefits of the latest thinking and research.

THE INTERNET AND E-LEARNING

It may well be that you are reading this material as part of an e-book. The ability of information and communication technology to support training and development is being exploited more and more.

From the 1990s onwards the practicality of on-line delivery and support for training and development programs has been increasing rapidly and the e-dimension to training and development strategies forms the subject of the next chapter of this material.

TIMELINE

» **c. 1400**: Development of guilds and apprenticeship. Foundation of early universities in Europe.
» **c. 1820**: Industrial Revolution leads to growth in in-house training. Mechanics' Institutes formed.
» **c. 1870**: Beginnings of compulsory primary (elementary) education.
» **1914**: President Woodrow Wilson sets up the Commission on National Aid to Vocational Education.
» **1930s**: Universal secondary education becomes the norm.
» **1939–45**: Second World War.
» **1969**: UK establishes the Open University.
» **1970s**: Studies into how adults learn.
» **1980s**: Growth in CPD mirrors rapid growth in technology.
» **1990s**: E-learning systems are developed.

KEY LEARNING POINTS

» The apprenticeship system allowed employers to link training and development to their business strategies.
» There has been a steady growth in vocational education, as the technological needs of commerce have increased.
» Continuous Professional Development is now a requirement for many jobs and professions.
» Academic institutions and organizations can gain considerable benefit through training and development partnerships.
» There has been growth in the use of the Internet to support training and development programs.

Training and Development Strategies and the E-Dimension

This chapter considers the role of Information and Communication Technology (ICT) in the development of a training and development strategy and includes:

» how ICT can assist in overcoming the barriers to training and development caused by distance and size;
» the role of ICT in providing access to research information;
» the use of simulations;
» the need for training in ICT use; and
» best practice.

The use of information and communication technology (ICT) to assist in the training and development process is now commonplace. This chapter considers the implications of the e-dimension for the opportunities it presents in defining a training and development strategy rather than for the mechanics of using ICT for training and development.

The key areas in which ICT can allow an organization to expand the horizons of its training and development strategy are those of distance, size, research, and simulation.

DISTANCE

In the ExpressExec titles *Managing Diversity* and *Training and Development Express* there is information on a highly successful partnership between British Airways and a number of academic institutions to deliver management training across the airline's global network.

In the 1990s, General Accident (now part of the Norwich Union insurance group) ran an annual management development week for selected members of staff across its global network.

In both the above cases there was a need for staff to travel, often long distances, to access at least part of the program. Traveling long distances to access training and development programs incurs not only the costs of the travel but also the opportunity costs that are incurred when a person is away from the normal workplace for some time.

There is no doubt that development programs benefit from face-to-face interactions between the members of the program. In the British Airways management development program mentioned above, the participants in each cohort met at central locations (London, New York, Delhi, Sydney and Johannesburg) five to seven times during the program for a one-day workshop. They also came together with other cohorts for a residential weekend in the UK. The rest of the program involved self-study using distance learning materials.

ICT through the use of e-mail, e-learning and video conferencing can diminish the barriers to training and development caused by distance. The University of the Highlands and Islands Millennium Institute in the North of Scotland links a series of colleges and learning centers in both the Scottish Islands and the Western Isles. By using video-conferencing and the Internet, students are able to speak to each other and their tutors. Not surprisingly, the ability to remove distance as an obstacle to training and development has attracted the interest of both private and public sector organizations. The Institute is able to offer a high quality management development program (validated by the UK Institute of Management) as either a company-based or public-access program. Small companies or those with staff scattered over the remote area of the Highlands and Islands can access development without incurring huge time and financial costs.

Realizing that not every home has a computer, Internet access, and video-conferencing facilities, the partners in the Institute have set up a network of tele-cottage style learning centers where the public can access training. Companies can buy time in these centers. The centers are linked to main sites of the Institute's partners where professional assistance and tuition are available.

As more and more organizations develop their own dedicated electronic networks, the less impact distance has on the delivery of training and development and greater flexibility is given to those who are devising strategy.

SIZE

One of the problems that besets small and even medium-sized organizations when considering training and development relates to economies of scale. Like many activities the greater the activity, the lower the relative cost. A large organization will find that the price for training and developing an individual drops as more individuals are placed on a particular program. In addition a large organization will find that there are economies of scale when it comes to customizing training and development programs that are put together by external providers.

Large organizations also find that it is easier to release an individual to undertake training and development, as there is more likely to be somebody available to cover his or her work for a short period.

One of the great advantages of development programs lies not only in the area of skills but also in the network of contacts that a development program can foster. The old saying that "it is not what you know but who you know" is very true today. An individual's contacts can be as important as his or her skills.

The use of ICT as part of the training and development strategy can be of assistance to organizations of all sizes. Smaller organizations can use ICT to provide training for one or two individuals using a computer-based training package or for simulations – see below. It may be possible for the individual to work on the package at home, which relieves the organization of having to release him or her during work hours.

The use of e-mail and video-conferencing using a PC-based camera system allows individuals in small organizations to link up with others who are undergoing similar training and development. This aids the generation of a network of contacts.

Large organizations can use the same technology to link up program participants across sites and even across continents, as will be described in Chapter 5.

More and more training and development providers are offering Internet-based training and development programs that allow the participant to work at his or her time, pace, and location. Organizations that pay for such programs for their employees need to ensure that what is being offered can be easily transferred into the individual's work situation.

SIMULATION

Up to quite recent times commercial airline pilots trained using actual aircraft. The development of flight simulators has meant that a qualified pilot transferring from one type of aircraft to another may not actually fly the new type until he or she takes it on his or her first commercial flight. The training is carried out in highly sophisticated flight simulators.

Whilst a flight simulator is a very expensive piece of equipment, it cannot be crashed and thus represents a very cost-effective means of training pilots to transfer from one aircraft model to another. A mistake in a flight simulator is embarrassing; a mistake on a real flight deck can be disastrous!

Flight simulators are at the upper end of using technology for simulation but there are more mundane uses for ICT. Computers are excellent at performing "what if" tasks. A manager can examine the results of certain actions on his or her department's budgets, for instance, using a computer package. Despite the artificiality of simulations, properly conducted they can approximate to real life not only in actions but also emotions. Pilots have been known to exit a flight simulator sweating – so realistic is the scenario.

Simulation means that the training and development strategy need not be inhibited by using expensive machinery etc. for training purposes with the attendant risk of accidents. Sooner or later the individual will need to perform in the real world, but he or she can use technology to practice.

RESEARCH

Development programs, especially those concerned with aspects of management or CPD (Continuous Professional Development, see Chapter 3) often require the participant to carry out research into relevant issues. Few organizations can afford to maintain large libraries. If the participant has easy access to a large public or university library, they may be able to use its facilities. It is unlikely that such a library will have instant access to news items, government reports, and company reports. One of the best places to find these is on the Internet.

The increasing ease of Internet access has been a boon to those conducting research. Even books are now available in an e-format as e-books. The case study at the end of this chapter considers how the ExpressExec series itself is being used to facilitate e-learning.

Organizations such as the car spares company Unipart (see the title *Training and Development Express* in the ExpressExec series) in the UK have developed "learning zones" where books are available, but there is also Internet access for the purposes of research to support training and development programs.

The wealth of government statistics and company information that can be found by searching the World Wide Web is growing all the time. It has never been easier to access research information and thus to have up-to-date information at one's fingertips.

TRAINING FOR ICT USE

The vast majority of those leaving school and entering employment today have received ICT training and whilst they may need training on organization-specific applications, they are likely to possess a basic knowledge of ICT. Older employees might not be as confident about the use of ICT. In *Online Learning Today* (2002), Heather Shea-Schultz and John Fogarty have commented on the need to remove "technophobia" as this can be a major barrier to the use of ICT as a learning resource. Their statistics show the importance of ICT in the learning process. In 2001 47% of US colleges and universities offered some form of learning using ICT with a prediction that this would rise to 90% by 2004. It was expected that individuals and organizations in the US would spend $2.2bn on ICT-supported learning by 2004.

Shea-Schultz and Fogarty have also stressed the importance of aesthetics in designing ICT-supported learning to make the package not only have excellent content, but also to be user-friendly. They argue that unless care is taken with the design then learners could well be put off from using the package no matter how excellent the content is.

ICT is just one of the components of successful training and development. Its major benefit is its ability to span distance, time, and reality (using simulations). There is no doubt that more and more use will be made of ICT in the future, especially as it can bridge the training opportunities gap that can exist between large and small organizations.

BEST PRACTICE

Capstone/SofTools

One of the issues in management development programs is the provision of high quality material that covers the concepts and practical applications of current business thinking. Whilst there are many, many books on business and management, what is often needed is easily accessible material that provides an overview of the particular subject together with sources for further investigation.

Whether you are using a traditional book or an e-book version of this material, it will have been published by Capstone, part of the global publishers John Wiley.

Capstone, based in Oxford, UK, was founded in 1996 by Mark Allin, Richard Burton, and entrepreneur and business author Richard Koch to publish accessible and entertaining business books designed to bring executives rapidly up to speed with cutting-edge business thinking. In

2000 it was announced that Wiley Europe (the largest subsidiary of the New York-based publisher John Wiley) had acquired a majority stake in Capstone. Allin and Burton continue to lead Capstone's operations.

ExpressExec is one of the most important Capstone products. The concept was to provide those in business with 3 million words of the latest management thinking in an easily accessible format. Initially the ExpressExec series comprised 100 titles divided into 10 modules, each module containing 10 titles of 30,000 words each. The material is available either in traditional book form (of a size that can easily slip into a jacket pocket) or as e-books that can be downloaded onto a PC or PDA.

The first titles were introduced in 2001 and in 2003 the series was extended with the introduction of an extra 20 titles covering Sales and Training and Development Express.

ExpressExec goes far beyond the traditional book as it provides an integrated product that includes Web-based support for the series with the ability to access relevant articles and the possibility of having the series feed directly into corporate Websites and intranets. This greatly eases accessibility to business ideas and concepts throughout an organization – the ideas, etc. are as close as the nearest computer terminal! No longer do participants on development programs and those who need to travel in the course of their job have to carry around heavy books; they can travel light and log on when they need to access the relevant materials.

As each title is written to the same basic formula and includes case studies from North America, Europe, and Asia, ExpressExec is a huge database of material suitable for supporting training and development programs. By including such a wide range of material that is easily accessible, ExpressExec allows an organization's training and development strategy to be more flexible as the problem of providing case material, concepts, and ideas is simplified. The organization is able to place the material on its own network for access by its employees.

One of the partners in the ExpressExec project is the UK company SofTools. SofTools was founded in 1998 to design and develop a software product that captured and made available best practice business methods through the desktop. It was initiated in response to a request from Nokia Mobile Phones where Andy Bruce (the founder of SofTools) was running management leadership programs on Nokia's behalf.

It became apparent that many organizations implementing change and developing new skills would welcome a means of easy access to business and management thinking to support their development programs. The first SofTools desktop product was subsequently transformed over a three-year period using input from a variety of clients and a close partnership with Andersen Consulting (now Accenture). The product incorporates key components of e-learning and knowledge management, but is more focused on the individual and team – what is it that they need to help them perform? – the concept of an Integrated Performance Support System.

SofTools and ExpressExec

Capstone were looking to diversify out of paper-only book sales into electronic media – in part driven by the need to find alternative revenue streams, but also by the desire to exploit significant opportunities in the rapidly expanding e-learning/knowledge management market space. By taking content traditionally made available in book form and making it available over the Web, Capstone (and John Wiley) was able to target individual consumers. It became apparent that the inclusion of the SofTools electronic business tools added value to the basic ExpressExec product. ExpressExec content is used to enhance the SofTools Web-based virtual consultant product. SofTools has also a Wiley-branded performance support system called ExpressExec AdVantage. Current clients using the electronic business reports include: Nokia, Centrica, Bayer, and Pitcher & Piano.

The ExpressExec AdVantage product is a Web-based performance support system that supports the individual or team in the task they are performing. It provides more than just business concepts as it links insights and ideas in the right format directly to the workflow. There are four key elements:

1 Business imperatives – visibility of the current issues that organizations are dealing with.
2 Method – interactive business templates that explain how key concepts should be applied and provide a structured approach that reflects best practice.

3 Ask-an-expert – access to the insights and ideas of experts, links to discussion forums, and business FAQs.
4 On-line business reports – general business concepts providing a common and complete business reference library.

iPSS

Whilst training or coaching may enable people to develop short-term skills, such skills rarely endure over the long term unless their application is actively supported back in the work situation. The focus should therefore be on the team or person performing the task by asking, "What do they need to enable them to perform to the best of their ability?" The answer to this question is rarely simple or singular – a number of components will need to be in place.

To address this issue, SofTools has created a Web-based integrated Performance Support System (iPSS) that enables business teams to consistently apply best-practice methods – such as business planning, risk management, or critical decision-making. The iPSS is seen as a Virtual Business Coach in that it is designed to:

1 teach the user about new techniques;
2 provide interactive templates for completing the task;
3 enable users to learn from each other and from the past; and
4 give senior managers greater visibility and control across remote or virtual teams.

In the current economic climate SofTools believes that iPSSs are no longer optional for survival – they are a necessity. By licensing the SofTools iPSS to leading training and consulting companies, the platform is used to address a variety of key issues currently facing modern businesses, for example: "how to make the sales force more effective at planning campaigns," "how to monitor and control operational projects," and "how to increase profit awareness at all levels of staff."

KEY LEARNING POINTS

» ICT can aid the development of a training and development strategy by overcoming the barriers of distance.

» Small organizations can use ICT to obtain contextualized training and to avoid staff losing work time.

» ICT provides means of accessing information quickly and easily whatever the location of the individual.

» ICT can facilitate simulation.

» The use of ICT itself as a training and development vehicle may require individuals to receive training in how to use it to its best advantage.

Implementing a Training and Development Strategy – Global Implications

This chapter considers the implications of global operations on the implementation of a training and development strategy and includes:

» globalization;
» thinking globally but acting locally;
» the 7Cs of global human resource management;
» the importance of culture within the 7Cs and thus within the training and development strategy; and
» best practice – Yum Restaurants International.

Globalization is the process whereby organizations offer their products and services on a global rather than a local basis.

As this process continues, organizations are having to consider the international dimension to their training and development plans and this obviously has implications for the training and development strategy from which those plans are derived.

As soon as an organization commences operations (as opposed to purely selling a product abroad) in countries other than its home country, it needs to take into account the differences in customs, legislation, educational standards, and employment practices. One of the major issues for any organization that commences global operations is the need to adapt to a new culture. Not only do the new employees need training and developing in the culture and practices of the organization, but existing employees will also need training and development in the culture of the new area of operations. British Airways, as a multinational organization, has for many years provided culture classes for those of its staff moving to a new part of the airline's global network so that they will not cause offense by their speech and behavior and will be able to understand the culture of their new colleagues. As this material was being prepared in November 2002, British Airways had undergone the same traumas as many other airlines following the terrorist attacks of 9/11. However in November 2002, BA was one of the few traditional global (as opposed to low-cost) airlines to have gone back into profit.

THINK GLOBAL BUT ACT LOCAL

Success in moving to a global operation is most likely when the organization "thinks globally but acts locally." The aim is to have all the benefits of brands, size, research etc. that large global organizations have but to somehow present an image of being indigenous to the particular region in question. Shell, Ford, Coca-Cola, Microsoft, and Kentucky Fried Chicken (part of the case study at the end of this chapter) are all, with the exception of Shell, which is a Netherlands-based organization, US companies. Notwithstanding the fact that most consumers know that these companies are not indigenous, they have local operations that are tailored to local needs and hence can engender local loyalties. This does not occur by accident. Local staff need training and development that reflects both the home and local values of the organization and those at corporate headquarters need training and development on local issues and local culture. There are important implications for the organization's training and development strategy. The strategy must be at the same time global but also reflect local needs. The strategy may well apply across the organization but how it is implemented can often be a function of local conditions.

George Yip (1992) has made the important point that opportunities for staff in regions outside the home region for the organization to receive training and development must be as available to them as they are to their colleagues at the home base. Failure to ensure this can lead to a lack of motivation and the danger that the service offered by the organization will not be consistent.

Pat Joynt and Bob Morton have edited a useful volume, *The Global HR Manager* (1999), which considers the issues that face those responsible for the HRM (Human Resource Management)/personnel function in organizations operating on a global stage. They have introduced what they call "the Seven Cs" of international HRM of which two – Competencies and Careers – have direct implications for an organization's training and development strategies and the remaining five indirect implications. The "Seven Cs" are:

» Culture
» Competition
» Communications
» Competencies – implications for training and development
» Compensation
» Careers – implications for training and development
» Collaboration.

Culture

Culture can be defined as the "way we do things around here" and differs from place to place across the globe, between ethnic groups and between organizations. There is, fortunately, a wealth of material on managing cultural differences and the reader is advised to consult the ExpressExec title *Managing Diversity* (Chapters 5 and 6) in this series, *Riding the Waves of Culture* by Fons Trompenaars, *When Cultures*

Collide by Richard D. Lewis and *Managing Cultural Differences* by Philip Harris and Robert Moran (details of these texts are given in Chapter 9). The quoted texts provide examples of how business is conducted in various cultures.

It would be a foolish organization that did not take account of the culture in which it was planning to operate. In respect of this material different cultures have different attitudes to training, development, and education and these will have implications for both the development and especially the implementation of a training and development strategy. The cultural differences that need to be taken into account include:

» **What form of hierarchies does the culture encourage?** In a particular culture it may be necessary to train a person higher up in the hierarchy before somebody lower down, not because that person needs the training or development first but because of his or her position. In a culture that is hierarchical a strategy that offers training and development to all employees may need to be adapted to train and develop those further up the hierarchy first. Whilst this may well go against equal opportunities policies it may be necessary in the short term. It will be important that senior staff in the new culture buy in to the training and development strategy, something they may resist if their position appears, to them, to be threatened.

» **Attitudes to gender**. Training and development should be provided in line with strict equal opportunities polices. In cases where the culture does not usually provide equal opportunities, the organization should be sensitive in the way that it explains why it intends to insist on equal opportunities being applied to all aspects of its operation and not just training and development. Good training and development can be very productive in helping to change attitudes and providing opportunities for development to those who might be denied such opportunities were it not for the fact that they were employed by the organization.

» **Attitudes to age and experience**. There may well be issues not only of the order in which employees are offered training and development opportunities, but also the age and experience of the deliverers of such programs. This can be a considerable issue in development programs where the focus is wider than just training for a particular task. Many US and European organizations provide management development programs to junior staff who show management potential. There are areas of the world where this would normally be unacceptable given the way hierarchies are arranged in those areas. There are still places where position depends on age rather than ability, although this is a practice that is declining. Sensitivity is required especially in convincing senior staff that providing development opportunities to their juniors should not be considered a threat to the senior person's position.

» **Attitudes to the education process**. If employees have been used to an education process that is formal and examination/test-based, they may not consider more informal training and development programs to carry much credibility. The training methods used may need to be adapted at first to correspond to what the trainees are used to. A consideration of the means by which training is to be implemented needs to form part of the strategy. The strategy should explain not only what is needed in the form of training and development, but also how it is to be provided and the rationale behind the choices.

It is not difficult to discover the cultural norms of an area and it is nearly always worth taking the time to do so. Training and development that can be related to the culture of an area is always going to have a better chance of succeeding than trying to use the programs and language from one area in another.

Competition

It has been stressed that training and development do not exist in a vacuum but that they should be tied to organizational strategies. Organizations train and develop their employees so that the organization can gain competitive advantage over others working in the same field.

An understanding of the competition and how competitors are training and developing their people is vital for the drawing up of a training and development strategy. In cases where an organization is moving into a new geographic area it is useful to consider how more established players in the market deal with training and development and what skills they believe are necessary at the present and will be necessary in the future.

Communications

A training and development strategy can often include components that not only develop the individual but also aid communication and networking across the organization. The development programs run by British Airways and General Accident mentioned at the beginning of this chapter had this as one of their objectives.

When an organization moves into a new region it is sensible to identify some key employees who can attend training and development sessions with existing employees.

Competencies – implications for training and development

All the staff of an organization, regardless of where they are based, need to be able to demonstrate the core competencies that the organization has deemed essential. One of the first steps an organization should take when moving into a new region is to put in place training and development based on the core competencies.

Organizations often find it useful to link training and development in core competencies with work on the organizational culture and aims as part of an induction package to the employees in the new area. The sooner these staff members "buy in" to the organization's values, the sooner the new operation will begin to make an effective contribution to the organization's operations.

Compensation

Compensation in HR terms refers to salaries and other benefits. Training and development, whether they lead to increased pay levels or not, have to benefit both the organization and the individual. The individual needs to see the personal benefit he or she will receive from the training and development. If organizations move into less developed economies, the benefits staff can receive from training and development opportunities can stretch beyond the organization and into their wider lives. In areas where further and higher education opportunities are limited, the benefits to the organization of having an effective training and development strategy can include the attraction of high quality staff. These people may well be motivated by the opportunity to access training and development as well as for the monetary compensation in the form of wages.

Careers – implications for training and development

Training and development should form a part of an individual's strategy for his or her career progression. Whilst new blood is always to be welcomed in an organization, it needs to be balanced by those employees who have progressed from within the organization. The latter will have a clear understanding of the organizational culture whilst the former bring fresh ideas and thinking. A balance between "picking your own" and "growing your own" is always to be desired.

Organizations moving into new areas will wish to engender employee loyalty and this can be assisted by a training and development strategy that presents the employee with a career development path within the organization.

Collaboration

Throughout the world there are colleges, universities, and training providers that know the local conditions. In the first instance an incoming organization can form productive partnerships with training and development providers. The organization can benefit from their local knowledge and local providers are likely to have more credibility with the new employees.

A further form of collaboration (and one that is discussed in greater detail in the next chapter) involves collaborative training and development activities conducted with both the organization's staff and staff from key suppliers and even customers. Training and development often provide opportunities for staff from suppliers and customers to work with the organization's staff in a relationship that is based on communal learning rather than commercial issues.

The arrival of an organization into an area may well be regarded with suspicion. However, if the organization shows that it will provide not only direct economic benefits to the area but will increase the training, development, and career prospects for local inhabitants then it is more likely to be welcomed. This benefit to the organization highlights the importance of the training and development strategy and its role within the overall expansion strategy of the organization.

BEST PRACTICE

Yum Restaurants International (YRI)

Whilst Yum Restaurants International might not be a household name, Pizza Hut and Kentucky Fried Chicken (KFC) most certainly are. By 2002 there were over 12,000 Pizza Huts and over 10,000 KFCs worldwide. In the first half of 2001 Yum Restaurants International, a Dallas, TX organization with five core branding concepts – Pizza Hut, KFC, Taco Bell, A&W All-American Food Restaurants, and Long John Silver – opened 378 traditional outlets. The parent company of the "Yum brands concept" is Tricon Global Restaurants Inc.

YRI operates in over 100 countries, and has more than 30,000 restaurants with annual sales in 2001 in excess of $22bn, up from $8bn in 1996. The operation is a blend of franchises and equity outlets with franchises predominating. With such a global spread the training and development strategy needs to have the maintenance of product and service consistency as one of its main aims.

Each of Yum Brands' concepts is engaged in the operation, development, franchising, and licensing of a system of both traditional and non-traditional fast-food outlets. Non-traditional units include express units and kiosks which have a more limited menu and operate in non-traditional locations such as gas stations, convenience stores, stadiums, amusement parks, and colleges, where a full-scale traditional outlet would not be practical or efficient. In addition, there are a number of outlets housing more than one concept (known as "2n1s"). Of these, approximately 354 units offer both the full KFC menu and a limited menu of Taco Bell products, and approximately 13 units offer both the full KFC menu and a limited menu of Pizza Hut products.

In each concept, consumers can either dine in or carry out food. In addition, Taco Bell and KFC offer a drive-thru option in many stores. Pizza Hut and, on a much more limited basis, KFC offer delivery service.

The success of the various operations relies on the preparation of food with high quality ingredients as well as unique recipes and special seasonings to provide appealing, tasty and attractive food at competitive prices.

A&W Restaurants began in 1919 in California with the sale of root beer whilst KFC dates from the 1930s when Colonel Harland Sanders opened his first roadside restaurant.

Long John Silver's is America's largest quick-service seafood chain with more than 1200 units worldwide. The concept was developed in 1968 and the first Long John Silver's Fish'n' Chips opened in 1969. Long John Silver's, whose name was inspired by Robert Louis Stevenson's classic *Treasure Island*, began with small wharfside buildings. The modern restaurants have updated exteriors that sport a stronger retail identity with bolder colors etc.

Pizza Hut began in 1958 when two college students from Wichita, KS – Frank and Dan Carney – opened a pizza parlor. Today, there are over 12,000 restaurants worldwide.

Taco Bell was started in California in 1962 by Glen Bell. Taco Bell was built on the heritage of Mexico and the tastes and attitudes of the American Southwest.

All of the brands operate a policy known as HWWT, which stands for How We Work Together, to recognize achievement. HWWT is based around eight precepts that stem from the core values of the organization. The concepts are:

» **Customer mania**: Listening and responding to the voice of the customer – being obsessed with going the extra mile to make the customer happy.
» **Belief in people**: Believing in people and trusting in positive intentions. Encouraging ideas from everyone, and actively developing a workforce that is diverse in style and background.
» **Recognition**: Celebrating the achievements of others and having fun doing it.
» **Coaching and support**: Coaching and supporting each other.
» **Accountability**: Giving people ownership of the tasks they carry out.
» **Excellence**: Taking pride in work and having a passion for excellence.
» **Positive energy**: Working positive energy and intensity to ensure that bureaucracy does not hinder the service to the customer.

» **Teamwork with productive conflict**: Using the positive aspects of conflict to move the team forward.

It is pleasant to see that an organization has fun as part of its core values. Fun and productivity are by no means mutually exclusive. It should also be noted that coaching is a core value – coaching and mentoring are important aspects of any training and development strategy. YRI also understand that providing training and development aids staff in "buying in" to the organization and thus increases motivation.

Those writing fiction use a concept known as the "suspension of disbelief." Cabot's Cove in *Murder, She Wrote* and Oxford, the English university city that is the setting for the *Inspector Morse* mysteries, seem very dangerous places indeed with one, two, or even more murders per story. We know that this is not the case in reality, but are prepared to suspend our disbelief in order to enjoy a good story. Thinking globally but acting locally involves a similar suspension of disbelief. If one visits the KFC in the main square of the city of Maastricht in the Netherlands, the menu is in Dutch, the staff are clearly local and yet the operation is American. The perception of the customer is that this is a local operation despite the knowledge that it is a US fast-food chain.

One of the competitive selling points of operations like these (Macdonald's is another example) is that there is consistency across the whole operation, and that requires considerable training of staff.

Across the organization there are those who are trained to be "CHAMPS" – a concept that is highly focused on customer service. In the fast-food sector the most important things to the customer are product quality and service. The product quality and customer service in this type of operation need to be the same whether the outlet is in Denver or Doncaster, Sydney or Seattle. One of the roles of the CHAMPS is to assist franchisees and managers in achieving consistency.

Not only are there product and training opportunities for staff, but also assistance with external studies if required. There are also management development opportunities. YRI policy is to train, develop and promote from within wherever possible. Training is for more effective task completion whereas the development is part of the process of career progression. Both are important.

As part of the rigorous selection process potential franchisees are required to complete an extensive training program as part of the selection process. This includes both in-store and classroom training sessions. The trainee must demonstrate proficiency at various stages in the training program. Franchisees who appoint a key operations director are required to complete an accelerated training course. YRI provides the Developing CHAMPIONS training curriculum for the training of Managers and Team Members. The franchisee pays all costs for Manager and Team Member training during start-up and the ongoing operation of the business.

YRI believe that by adhering to YRI methods for operations and training, the franchisee will strengthen his or her own business, build equity in the brand, and help build the profitability of the enterprise. This statement enhances the status of training.

Whilst a traditional view of fast-food operations centers on low pay, low skills, and temporary staff, it is a fact that customers have become more discerning as regards to product quality, service, and consistency. The YRI operation and the importance it gives to training reflects this.

KEY INSIGHTS

» Global operations need consistency of product and service.
» Franchise operations can use training as part of the franchisee selection process.
» Providing training and development aids staff in "buying in" to the organization and thus increases motivation.
» Both training in specific tasks and wider development should be provided.
» Training and development can assist in promoting from within.

The State of the Art of Implementing Training and Development Strategies

This chapter considers the state of the art of implementing training and development strategies. It includes:

» reasons for training and development;
» costs and benefits;
» the training and development cycle;
» core competencies;
» defining objectives;
» training needs analysis;
» training to improve performance;
» training and development as change agents;
» training and development facilitating empowerment;
» training and development and recruitment and retention;

» training and development for suppliers and customers;
» the learning organization;
» putting the strategy together;
» implementing the strategy; and
» training the trainers.

"Knowledge is the critical factor for all organizations"
Jim Kouzes

REASONS FOR TRAINING AND DEVELOPMENT

The reasons that organizations need to train and develop staff are:

» to do current tasks better;
» to be able to do future tasks;
» to develop and retain people to grow with the organization; and
» to attract high caliber people into the organization.

All of these aspects need to be included in the organization's training
and development strategy.

TRAINING TO OVERCOME PERFORMANCE PROBLEMS

Training and development should always be seen as positive business
activities. Negativity is a danger when training is put in place to
help remedy an individual's performance problems. There are those
individuals who are either incompetent, lazy, or lack the aptitude for
certain tasks. It is legitimate to ask why they were ever employed in the
first place. If, on the other hand, an individual is having performance
problems due to a lack of training in the requisite skills, it is beholden
on the organization to provide the necessary training. If there is then no
improvement, the organization will have a legitimate right to institute
disciplinary procedures. Unfortunately there are still cases where it is
a lack of training rather than any fault of the individual that causes
problems and the individual is let go with the result that a potentially
valuable employee is lost to the organization.

Training should never be seen as a punishment. If it is so perceived
it will be entered into half-heartedly. It is also important that the
implementation of any training program – but especially one designed
to address a performance problem – is flexible enough to accommodate
the various different learning styles of individuals. Learning styles do
not form part of the development and implementation of a training and
development strategy; rather they are tactical in nature. However, the

strategy should be such as to allow trainers to use methods appropriate to the individual. The work of Kolb (1974) and Honey and Mumford (1982 and 1986) should be consulted in this respect – see Chapter 8. A description of the work of Kolb and Honey and Mumford can be found in chapter 6 of *Training and Development Express* in this series. The strategy should not dictate how training and development are to be carried out, as this will depend on individual trainers, individual employees, and the circumstances at the time. The strategy is about what needs to be done whilst the actual training itself is tactical.

The first part of developing a strategy is concerned with considering the overall strategy and goals of the organization and then identifying the training needs to meet what the organization wishes to do.

The second phase is involved with the formulation of plans to meet the identified training needs. The third phase is a consideration of the practicalities of implementing the training and development whilst the fourth phase is the evaluation of the training and development provided. Paradoxically, whilst the evaluation is the final phase, the formulation of the success criteria is part of the first and second phases. It is impossible to say that something is a success unless the success criteria were laid out at the very beginning.

COSTS AND BENEFITS

Richard Pettinger, the UK-based writer on human resources and general management topics, has considered some of the reasons why organizations do not undertake the training they should and why much training is often ineffective. In *Mastering Employee Relations* (2002), he comments that for many organizations training and development are seen as costs to be borne rather than investments to be made. He further comments that too many organizations load the responsibility for training and development onto already overworked front-line staff. He concludes that this lack of status and resources for training and development explains why employees do not always value training and development opportunities. He notes, correctly although unfortunately, that training budgets are often the first to be cut in times of crisis. In the early 1990s, at the time of the Gulf War, airlines had a similar downturn in sales as that following September 11, 2001. Many of them slashed their training budgets. British Airways did not and reaped considerable benefit in the following years as they had trained staff with high morale able to capitalize on the upturn in air travel following the end of the conflict. As was noted in the last chapter, BA has been one of the first of the global carriers to show a recovery after the events of September 11, 2001.

The training and development strategy should be worded in such a manner as to leave no doubt that it is seen as an investment and one of considerable potential benefit to both the organization and the individual.

THE TRAINING AND DEVELOPMENT CYCLE

The process is not linear, but cyclical, as shown in Chapter 2 of this material.

This chapter, indeed this material, is not concerned with the practical implementation of training and development but with the strategies that have led the organization to use the chosen methods of implantation. Details of practical training and development techniques can be found in other ExpressExec titles.

TRAINING AND DEVELOPMENT AS PART OF AN OVERALL STRATEGY

The fact that an organization's training and development strategy needs to be an integral part of the overall strategy of the organization has been stressed throughout this material. Those responsible for the formulation of the training and development strategy should begin their task by reviewing the overall strategy and asking some simple questions as listed below.

If this is what the organization wants to do:

» "Can we do it using our existing skills base without any training and development?"

If the answer is no, then:

» "What additional skills do we need in our skills base in order to move in the required strategic direction?"

and,

» ''How are those skills to be acquired?''

There are three basic methods that an organization can use to acquire skills:

1 train existing employees;
2 recruit new employees who already possess the required skills; or
3 outsource the operation or process that requires the skills.

Option 3, outsourcing, does not require the organization to undertake any training or development, but does leave the organization in a position where it may be vulnerable, as it will be losing some control over the operation and process.

SETTING THE OBJECTIVES FOR TRAINING AND DEVELOPMENT

The training and development strategy should have the aim of:

ensuring that the skill base of the organization is such that the organization can fulfill the objectives of its overall strategy and that all employees possess the core competencies/capabilities required by the organization.

In a similar vein, the financial strategy of an organization should have the aim of ensuring that the organization has sufficient financial resources to fulfill its objectives. Marketing and sales will have similar aims in respect of customers.

CORE COMPETENCIES/CAPABILITIES

Mayo (1998) defines core competencies (or core capabilities, depending on the terms used by the organization) as those skills that represent the fundamental expertise within the organization. Some core competencies such as people skills, analytical skills, customer service, numeracy, and literacy etc. are generic to all organizations, whilst there are also technical core competencies that are organization-specific. Core competencies represent the expertise that allows the organization to compete in the chosen field.

Any training and development strategy should have the development of core competencies as a fundamental objective. Core competencies are not static, but dynamic, and change as the organization and its environment change. The training and development strategy needs to recognize that there should be a continual process of core competence development for all staff.

Generic core competencies such as people skills and customer service skills need to reflect the values, attitudes, and beliefs of the organization – collectively referred to as the culture of the organization.

It has become a practice in many organizations to develop a set of core competencies for the organization and to seek to evaluate the degree to which individuals can demonstrate them. Such an activity provides a useful link between training and development and the review of an individual's performance through the appraisal process.

DEFINING TRAINING AND DEVELOPMENT OBJECTIVES

The objectives to fulfill the training and development strategy should be defined in the manner that has become accepted for all business objectives – they should be defined in SMART criteria, i.e. they should be:

» Specific
» Measurable
» Agreed
» Realistic
» Time bound.

Each objective should be clearly specific so that those involved with its achievement know exactly what the objective is and how it relates to the overall strategy of the organization.

Secondly, it is important to state at the outset how the achievement of the objective is to be measured. Objectives need to be agreed by all concerned and should be realistic – i.e. achievable – and lastly time scales need to be set down. In 1999 the writer of this material argued that there should be an addition to SMART with it becoming C-SMART, the C standing for Customer-centered. The argument is that as the customer is the most important person in any organization, everything that the organization does should be centered around customer needs and wants. In the case of training and development, there will be two sets of customers to consider – the external customer and the internal customer. The latter will include individuals and departments that receive and benefit from the training and development.

The introduction of a new product range may lead to the setting of a training and development objective as shown in the following example (note: for the purposes of demonstrating C-SMART, a single example of a training and development objective is used for demonstration purposes):

EXAMPLE

An organization has an overall strategy of gaining increased market share in a particular market. The way it intends to do this is by introducing a new product – product X – into that market in six months' time. This will give rise to a training need for customer advisors. The training and development objective is therefore:

» To ensure that all customer advisors are trained to advise customers on the use of product X.

Setting this into C-SMART criteria is shown below:

Customer-centered

With the introduction of product X it is recognized that customers may need extra assistance in integrating the product into their current operation.

Specific

By the end of the training program all customer advisors will have the relevant knowledge to enable them to advise customers on how to set up product X and integrate it into their operations.

Measurable

By the end of the training the individual will be able to demonstrate clearly how product X can be integrated into the customer's current operation by explaining each of the functions of product X.

Agreed

The training program is being developed with inputs from both the customer advisors and representatives of the department developing the product.

Realistic

After discussion with the customer advisors and the managers of the department developing product X, the training program will also include extra training on system Y, as this is an area that is likely to cause the most problems to customers. Customer advisors have expressed the opinion that this extra training is necessary.

Time bound

Product X is due to be placed in the market in six months, therefore all training is to be completed within five months, two weeks.

The training and development strategy will produce a series of training and development objectives.

TRAINING NEEDS ANALYSIS

In order to formulate an effective strategy, a starting point must be defined. The most obvious starting point is the current skills base of the organization. This can then be compared with the current required skills base and then the predicted skills base for the future. The process for analyzing the skills base is known as a Training Needs Analysis (TNA) and can be defined as a systematic review of the current skills base against organizational requirements in order to identify the skills gap.

A TNA should form the first step of implementing the training and development strategy. TNAs are often performed by external agencies that are contracted by the organization. Data on job practices, trends etc. are collected together with details of the skills present within the organization. This information then needs to be compared with the skills and knowledge needed at the present time (if an effective strategy has been followed in the past, there should only be minor mismatches) and what will be needed in the future.

Once the information has been collated, department and individual training and development plans can be devised and agreed with the relevant stakeholders.

At the same time, the organization will need to consider how the training and development are to be provided – by the organization, by an outside institution, on site, off site, during the day, by distance learning etc. Such decisions are tactical rather than strategic and cannot be made until the skills gap has been identified as part of the strategy process.

Tom Boydell and Malcolm Leary (1996) have identified three facets of performance within organizations:

1 doing things well, i.e. implementing;
2 doing things better, i.e. improving; and
3 doing new and better things, i.e. innovating.

The training and development strategy needs to consider all three of the above.

TRAINING AND DEVELOPMENT AS CHANGE AGENTS

Doing new and better things (see above) requires those involved to accept and benefit from change. Change almost always requires people to do something new, and this often means that they need to acquire new skills. Training and development strategies need to recognize the fear that change can produce – a fear that is often caused by the individual asking, "Can I actually do this?" Training needs to precede change and then run alongside it. If training only follows change it will involve a constant process of trying to catch up. Training before and during change can help alleviate fear and build confidence; training that is only implemented after the change begins is likely to increase fear and lead to a loss of individual confidence.

Jim Stewart (1991) believes that the role of the trainer is not just to provide skills but also to act as a change agent. To do this, trainers need a clear understanding of the direction the organization is heading in so that their work can be proactive rather than reactive. Stewart sees training and development as a major avenue for the management of the change process.

TRAINING AND DEVELOPMENT FACILITATING EMPOWERMENT

Empowerment is the process of releasing the full potential of employees in order for them to take on greater responsibility and authority in the decision-making process and providing the resources for this process to occur. The greater the individual's skills, the easier it is for the organization to empower that individual. Empowerment does not rely on skills alone. The individual needs confidence in his or her own ability and a belief that the organization will provide the necessary physical and emotional support. Development programs often have empowerment as a by-product. As the individual goes through a development program, he or she gains greater knowledge and usually wishes for opportunities to use the new knowledge and skills. He or she is likely to demand empowerment and a sensible organization should acquiesce, as we all do better when we believe we are empowered and have ownership.

Mentoring and coaching are seen by many, including Kenneth L Murrell and Mimi Meredith, as important parts of the empowerment process. They are an important part of the link between training and development and empowerment. Bill Ginnodo (1997) points out that facilitating and coaching are more effective than directing and controlling. The former are partnerships, the latter one-way relationships. People usually learn more in a partnership than in an ''us and them'' relationship. He also makes the very valid point that nothing is more empowering than providing employees with skills training to do their jobs well. It should be added that this is not just empowering, but also rewarding to the organization and the employee.

TRAINING AND DEVELOPMENT AND RECRUITMENT AND RETENTION

The concept of training and development as an investment has already been covered in this chapter. Bruce Tulgan, the author of *Winning the Talent Wars* (2001), has stressed the contribution training and development can make to recruiting and retaining talent within an organization. Organizations that invest in their employees are seen as good places to work due to the positive relationship such investment implies. Managers who look beyond the current job a person is doing and who then provide training and development opportunities for that individual are showing a commitment to the individual's future.

Tulgan comments on the lament of many managers – "We've spent all this money training this individual and now they've left for another company." This happens, but organizations that invest in their people are more likely to retain them and also to attract higher caliber applicants for positions.

A key part of a training and development strategy has to address the question, "How can we ensure that the skills etc. that an individual has gained through training and development are disseminated for the benefit of the whole organization?" A small company in the UK county of Oxfordshire used to encourage those who had attended training to give briefings on what they had learnt to their colleagues. They also encouraged mentoring and coaching so that skills could be passed on and thus retained within the organization.

TRAINING AND DEVELOPMENT FOR SUPPLIERS AND CUSTOMERS

Whilst the majority of training and development involves the staff of the organization, there are two other constituencies that can also benefit.

It may be considered beneficial to involve key suppliers in certain of the organization's training and development programs in order to promote understanding and increase efficiency. Major automobile manufacturers have adopted such a strategy in order to aid quality assurance. In the 1990s, British Airways operated a special one-day program entitled "Winning for Customers" that involved every single one of their employees. In addition, key suppliers were also invited to send members of their staff so that there would be a greater understanding of what the airline was trying to achieve with its service standards.

It may also be beneficial to provide training and development for customers. Microsoft Windows® comes with a tuition package as part of the help function. Aircraft manufacturers have always offered training for customers. They have a vested interest in ensuring that the pilots of their customers are as competent as possible. Both the airline itself and the airframe manufacturer suffer bad publicity when there is an accident.

THE LEARNING ORGANIZATION

The quote at the beginning of this chapter is from Jim Kouzes, the President of the Tom Peters Group/Learning Systems and the co-author of *The Leadership Challenge* (1987) and *Credibility* (1995). Peter Kline and Bernard Saunders (1993) believe that the difference between organizational learning and the learning of an individual is that whilst the individual stores knowledge in his or her brain, organizations store it in their cultures. Anthropologists would agree with this view of learning as human groups, races, nations etc. also store knowledge in their cultures where it is accessible to others who can understand the culture. The manifestation of learning is seen in the products, services, and documentation of the organization as well as in the behavior of employees.

All organizations, with the exception of the most unsuccessful, learn. A learning organization, however, is one that according to Kline and Saunders "learns on its own quite apart from the many individual learnings that also take place within it." Jim Stewart (1991) has defined a learning organization as one that not only facilitates the learning of all its members (employees), but also continuously transforms itself in the process. It can be seen that employees in a learning organization do not just attend a course and gain personal benefit. Their learning is then absorbed into the organization to form part of the organizational knowledge base. D.A. Gavin (1993) has described a learning organization in terms of its skill in creating, acquiring, and transferring knowledge, and at modifying its behavior to reflect new knowledge and insights. A learning organization works with its employees to ensure that both parties gain from training and development opportunities. It might be thought that all organizations would adopt this approach given its obvious mutual advantages. The fact is that whilst there are more and more learning organizations, there are still those that seem to decouple individuals and learning organizations. The loss of a key staff member is usually less of an issue for learning organizations as, whilst the person might leave, much of his or her knowledge remains. The term "learning organization" is relatively recent, but the concept is quite old. The apprenticeship system (see Chapter 3), whereby an older worker near to retirement trained up an apprentice and passed on many years of knowledge and experience, equates to the idea of a learning organization.

The ExpressExec title *The Learning Organization* provides an in-depth coverage of the topic. MTR, the mass transit operator in Hong Kong and the feature of a case study in Chapter 7, considers it important that it projects itself as a learning organization.

PUTTING THE STRATEGY TOGETHER

The strategy needs to be developed with all the stakeholders involved, as this will aid the implementation process that is the subject of the next section.

It is important that the strategy answers the following questions.

» Why is this strategy necessary?
» How does it fit in with the overall business strategy?
» What forms should the training and development take?
» Who are the stakeholders?
» What are the success criteria?
» Where within the organization do implementation and management lie?

IMPLEMENTING THE STRATEGY

The responsibility for implementation of a training and development strategy will differ from organization to organization. A simplistic answer to where the responsibility should lie might be thought to be the human resource (HR)/training department. The correct answer is more complex than that. If all the responsibility for implementation is vested in the HR or training department, then managers in other departments may be tempted to conclude that they have no role.

The HR or training department may well be responsible for the actual sourcing and delivery of the training, but the content and evaluation should be a partnership between the HR/training department, the line managers of the trainees, and the trainees themselves. All three need to "buy in" to the training. It is of special importance that line managers buy in to the development programs undertaken by their staff as these are usually of a longer duration and require the individual to analyze and challenge current practices. It is important that his or her line manager does not find this threatening.

One of the issues that was confronted by the public sectors in the US and the UK during the Reagan/Thatcher years was that of distinguishing between the responsibility to ensure that services were delivered and the responsibility for the actual delivery. The Reagan/Thatcher philosophy was that the government and its agencies did not have to actually deliver health, education etc. directly, but it was responsible for seeing that the services were delivered and to an agreed standard. It was this philosophy that led to the privatization of many UK services including power, railways, and telecommunications. In the US, as Desmond King (1987) has commented, President Reagan began by increasing the power of the State's legislators *vis-à-vis* the federal government. Right wing administrations tend to "roll back the state," whilst the left of center has had a tendency to centralize provision in its hands. The Labor administration of Tony Blair from 1997 in the UK has somewhat shattered the conventional view of how a left of center administration behaves by carrying on with the privatization policies begun under Thatcher. It is interesting to note the close relationship between Blair and President George Bush as the UK Labour (*sic*) Party and the Republicans had not been regarded as natural bedfellows in the past.

The HR/training department faces similar issues – is it responsible for seeing that the necessary training and development occurs, but also does it have a responsibility for delivery? In all but the largest of organizations the expertise to conduct training may not be present in the organization and it will be necessary to form partnerships with external providers. The case study on "The Famous Grouse" in the next chapter gives an example of shared delivery with an outside consultancy being brought in for a particular aspect of training.

The decision as to whether the success criteria have been met cannot but involve the line managers of those being trained and developed. These are the people who will be able to see how performance has improved.

TRAINING THE TRAINERS

The training and development strategy needs to address not only physical and financial resources, but also the training and development needs of those training and developing staff. A large organization may have a number of qualified "professional trainers," but managers and other colleagues may well be needed as coaches and mentors, and there will also be a need for coaches and mentors from the general work force. These people need training and developing for their role if they are to be successful and add value to the training and development process.

In summary, the training and development strategy is not concerned with the actual delivery, but with the rationale, framework, and resources that support the delivery of training and development programs that are themselves derived from the overall organizational strategy.

KEY LEARNING POINTS

» Training is carried out so that those in the organization are able to do current tasks better, are prepared for future tasks and so that the organization can develop and retain people to grow with the organization, and to attract high caliber people into the organization.

» Training should be the first area considered when examining an individual's performance problems.

» The analysis of training needs to highlight any gaps is an important part of the development of the training and development strategy.

» Core competencies (or core capabilities depending on the terms used by the organization) are those skills that represent the fundamental expertise within the organization.
» Training and development objectives should be in C-SMART criteria.
» Training and development objectives are linked to the overall business objectives.
» Training and development is an important component in the change process.
» Training and development can be used to empower people.
» Mentoring and coaching are less formal but highly effective support mechanisms for training and development.
» The role of training and development in attracting and retaining high caliber, talented people should not be underestimated.
» Training and development may be extended to key suppliers and customers.
» Learning organizations embrace a culture of training and development.
» Mentors and trainers are not born – they need training for their role.

In Practice – Implementing Training and Development Strategy Success Stories

This chapter contains case studies on three organizations that have developed and implemented successful training and development strategies.

The three organizations are:

» Kodak;
» The "Famous Grouse" Experience; and
» Hong Kong MTR.

KODAK

Kodak is a name recognized across the globe and is almost synonymous with photography. George Eastman, the founder of Kodak, was born 1854 in upstate New York. Leaving school at 14, Eastman had little grounding in science and technology.

The 1860s saw a considerable growth in what was then the new art (and science) of photography. Ward et al. (1990) comment on the "boom" in photography during the US Civil War of 1861–65 as official photographs of the battle sites were commissioned and soldiers on both sides sat for personal studies to give to their loved ones.

In 1884 Eastman patented the first film in roll form to prove practicable; in 1888 he perfected the Kodak camera, the first camera designed specifically for roll film. It is believed that he just made up the name Kodak. In 1892 he established the Eastman Kodak Company, at Rochester, NY, one of the first firms to mass-produce standardized photography equipment. This company also manufactured the flexible transparent film, devised by Eastman in 1889, which proved vital to the subsequent development of the motion picture industry, an industry that was to grow in leaps and bounds in the early years of the twentieth century. Eastman was associated with the company in an administrative and an executive capacity until his death in 1932. Eastman was one of the outstanding philanthropists of his time, donating more than US$75mn to various projects. Notable among his contributions were a gift to the Massachusetts Institute of Technology and endowments for the establishment of the Eastman School of Music in 1918 and of a school of medicine and dentistry at the University of Rochester in 1921.

Kodak, as a company, invests very heavily in its human resource. The investment in its people is seen as an integral part of the company's strategy of remaining in the forefront of the photographic and allied industries.

Kodak operates a huge range of development programs and training opportunities. This case study considers two of these in particular. In addition to programs for existing staff, Kodak also provides internships for students. These internships generally last for 10 weeks and are available to those registered on relevant degree programs from bachelor degrees to doctorates.

A core value stated by Kodak is the respect, integrity, and opportunities provided for personal development within the organization. Each employee at Kodak works with his or her supervisor or manager to develop an Employee Development Plan (EDP). The EDP is designed to assist the employee in meeting personal goals within the context of the business needs of Kodak.

The two examples below are based on Kodak Rotational Programs, first for engineers and secondly for image science. A similar rotational program is available for those concerned with software research, development, and production.

The Kodak Global Manufacturing Rotation Program (GMRP)

This program provides an opportunity for staff with an engineering degree and up to three years' experience in one of the following disciplines: mechanical, chemical, electrical, industrial, or manufacturing. The program is designed to develop future technical and manufacturing leaders by offering manufacturing-focused learning, consisting of both formal and also experiential learning events. The objectives of these learning events are to:

» broaden the individual's understanding of Kodak's business opportunities;
» establish a personal network of resources to support the individual's career; and
» enhance the individual's social and leadership skills.

The GMRP consists of a personalized employee development plan, job assignments, events, and classes.

Personalized employee development plan

This plan is intended to assist the individual to develop the skills and competencies necessary to succeed in Global Manufacturing at Kodak, including core and specialized training based on individual areas of interest and specific assignments. Core training includes:

» a general Kodak orientation;
» manufacturing process overview through tours and training;

» quality, reliability and lean manufacturing;
» education on Kodak processes; and
» people and leadership skills.

Job assignments

A series of job assignments enables the individual to develop and apply the skills necessary for effective technical contributions and manufacturing leadership. Each assignment is in a different technology or business so that all participants experience diverse Global Manufacturing opportunities. Assignments increase in complexity, opportunity, responsibility and accountability over time. Participants select assignments with advice and support from mentors and GMRP managers.

Events and classes

Formal training is provided using specific events and classes. These form an integral part of the program.

The Image Science Career Development (ISCD) Program

At Kodak, infoimaging (the combination of imaging science – cameras, scanners etc.–with ICT) is seen as an important part of the future strategy of the company.

The Image Science Career Development (ISCD) Program is designed for new hires at graduate level to connect the knowledge of their specific discipline with the hands-on application of newly acquired fundamental imaging science concepts to meet the challenges of the imaging industry.

The ISCD Program is a two-year program within Kodak's R&D organization in Rochester, NY, and is designed to develop imaging scientists and imaging engineers.

The core curriculum covers both traditional and digital imaging technologies. In addition to the imaging-focused courses, systems engineering, statistics, design of experiments, modeling, simulation, project management principles, and leadership courses assist in rounding out the broad scope of skills required to be successful in an imaging-related career. The courses are designed for individuals who will be primary contributors to engineering and development of current imaging systems.

Courses are provided by both Kodak staff and tutors from local educational establishments. Individual participants are also allocated a personal mentor.

Networks

Another component of the Kodak training and development strategy is the formation of a series of employee networks. These networks include the "Empower Network" designed to assist employees with disabilities enhance their skills, knowledge, and abilities and the "Asia-Pacific Exchange" (APEX) to aid recruitment and retention of Asian and Pacific Islands employees.

The whole philosophy of training and development at Kodak is based on mutual benefits for both the company and the individual. The rotation concept not only provides development opportunities for the individual participants, but also invigorates the organization as the individuals bring their increasing experience and expertise to different areas of the corporate operation.

Kodak maintains close links with colleges and universities (following the tradition set by George Eastman). By doing so the company is able to tap into the knowledge and expertise in the universities and provide additional educational opportunities for Kodak employees.

In all the training and development offered at Kodak it is possible to trace a direct link with the overall strategy of the company and its desire to be at the cutting edge of technology – a desire that means an investment in people as well as machinery.

KODAK TIMELINE

» **1854**: George Eastman born.
» **1868**: Eastman leaves school aged 14.
» **1880**: Eastman invents and patents the dry plate technique for photography in Rochester, NY.
» **1885**: Eastman film introduced to the market. Eastman markets the film not only in the US but also in London.

» **1888**: Eastman invents the name Kodak for his company.
» **1895**: First Kodak pocket camera.
» **1897**: Eastman begins to market in France.
» **1898**: Folding pocket camera introduced.
» **1907**: Global workforce – 5000.
» **1923**: Kodak introduce home cine film.
» **1924**: Eastman donates $30mn to US educational establishments including Rochester (NY) University and MIT.
» **1927**: Global workforce–20,000.
» **1932**: Death of George Eastman.
» **1934**: 35 mm film introduced.
» **1947**: Kodak begin to manufacture TV cameras.
» **1972**: Instamatic "pocket" cameras introduced.
» **1975**: 25 millionth Instamatic sold. Sales revenue for the Instamatic is over $4bn.
» **1984**: Kodak produce floppy discs for computers and VHS and Betamax video cassette tapes.
» **1990**: Photo CD introduced.
» **1991**: Writeable CDs introduced.
» **1999**: 250 millionth "one time use" camera recycled.
» **2002**: Kodak provides $2mn for scholarships for minority students.

KEY INSIGHTS

» Training and development are valued because they are part of the Kodak culture.
» There are clear links between the training and development strategy and the overall strategy of the organization.
» Training and development is not just about courses, but also includes job rotation schemes.
» Mentoring is an important part of training and development.
» Links with universities are valued.

THE "FAMOUS GROUSE" EXPERIENCE

The Famous Grouse is the brand name of one of the world's most popular whiskies. It is a genuine Scotch whisky as can be seen by the spelling - had it come from that other great home of whiskey - Ireland - it would have been spelt with an "e."

Highland Distillers, the distillers of The Famous Grouse, is headquartered in the ancient capital of Scotland - Perth - and is part of The Edrington Group, based in Glasgow, Scotland, from where the Group directs the international sales and marketing of its premium Scotch whisky brands. Best known amongst these are The Famous Grouse, Cutty Sark, and The Macallan Single Highland Malt (note that it is The Macallan and not just Macallan).

The Edrington Group owns and operates seven malt whisky distilleries: Glenrothes, Macallan, and Tamdhu on Speyside; Bunnahabhain on Islay; Highland Park on Orkney; Glenturret in Perthshire; and Glengoyne in the Highland region.

The Edrington Group's business is world-wide in its impact but based entirely in Scotland, where it covers the whole spectrum of the Scotch whisky industry, from cask to glass, through strategic partnerships in global distribution to the international marketing of its brands to the final consumer.

The origins of The Edrington Group, today one of the largest companies in the Scotch whisky industry, stretch back to the 1850s when the company was founded in Glasgow by the Robertson family. Edrington continues to operate with the Robertson family values of Integrity, Independence, Involvement and Innovation.

The Robertson family was also responsible for founding Highland Distillers back in 1887 and in the fall of 1999, Edrington acquired Highland along with its Famous Grouse, The Macallan, and Highland Park brands.

The Robertson Trust

This is a charitable trust funded to a considerable degree by dividend income from The Edrington Group and is charged with supporting a wide variety of charitable causes, largely in Scotland. In the last five years the Trust has given over £20mn to charities.

Glenturret and The Famous Grouse Experience

Whisky is a major source of income to the Scottish economy, not only through worldwide sales but also through its role in the tourist industry. Visitors to Scotland comprise both whisky connoisseurs and those whose knowledge of the drink may well be very limited. The interest in the national drink has spawned a thriving tourist sector for the distilling industry with a number of distilleries operating guided tours. Different areas of Scotland produce their own single and double malts, the taste reflecting the nature of the countryside in the area. There are in fact over 300 different Scotch whiskies. There is also whiskey (note the different spelling) produced in Ireland and even Japan. A visit to a distillery is almost obligatory for the visitor to Scotland.

The Glenturret Distillery was founded in 1775 and claims the title of the oldest distillery in Scotland. The distillery lies just outside the ancient market town of Crieff in Strathearn on the road from Perth to Oban. One of Crieff's claims to fame is that it was the site of Charles Edward Stuart's (Bonnie Prince Charlie's) last war council before his defeat at the battle of Culloden in 1746. The distillery is set on the banks of the quick-flowing Turret Burn, which rises on Benchonzie, flows into Loch Turret and thence to the River Earn just a few miles below the distillery. Whisky distilling requires a good supply of clean water and the Turret Burn provides that.

The location of the distillery set, as it is, amongst woods with the soothing sounds of both water and birds nearby could not be bettered as a tourist attraction – its main function today. The customer base as a tourist attraction includes not only those using their own or hire cars, but also a considerable number of coach parties. Glenturret has been operating as a visitor attraction for a number of years but its transformation into the award-winning Famous Grouse Experience is very recent.

The distillery ceased operation in 1921 and production was not restarted until the late 1950s. Cointreau, the French liqueur company, purchased Glenturret in 1981, the year after the site was opened to visitors. Glenturret was acquired by Highland Distillers in 1990.

The origins of the Famous Grouse brand can be traced back to the "Grouse Brand" developed by the Gloag Company in 1896. Matthew Gloag's daughter Phillipa is credited with designing the Grouse Brand label. The red grouse (*Lagopus lagopus scoticus*) is one of Scotland's best-known game birds. By the 1960s 25,000 cases were being produced, a figure that had risen to over one million by 1979 and 2.5 million by 2002. By 1980 "The Famous Grouse," as the brand was by then called, was the brand leader for blended whiskies in Scotland. Unlike the single malts, blended whisky contains a number of different whiskies carefully blended together. The Famous Grouse is not produced at Glenturret – the distillery produces up to 500,000 liters of the Glenturret single malt per annum, with part of the production going into the blend that makes up The Famous Grouse. Two percent of all production of any whisky is lost to evaporation and is known as "the Angel's share."

Whilst whisky production and sales remain the main focus of The Edrington Group's operation, the distilleries are important parts of the Scottish tourist economy. Over 21,000 visitors per annum has been quite normal for Glenturret with the distillery hosting over 2000 in the height of the season.

By the end of the 1990s, distillery tours were growing in number throughout Scotland but were often just that – a guided tour of the distillery. Except to the "whisky buff," if you had seen one distillery then you had seen them all. This has not been the case since the opening of The Famous Grouse Experience at the Glenturret distillery in 2002. The Experience is more than just a tour of the distillery, being an interactive experience utilizing a number of the senses.

Costing $4mn, The Famous Grouse Experience won a coveted BAFTA award – the British Academy of Film and Television Arts 2002 Interactive Entertainment Award – in the Sports and Leisure category. The interactive show, created by Land Design Studio in London and Art + Com in Berlin, takes visitors into the heart of the Famous Grouse brand to break new ground in the Scotch whisky industry by turning the traditional distillery tour into a truly interactive experience.

Ninety-seven percent of visitors have rated the interactive tour as "exceptional." It should be noted that visitors to The Famous Grouse Experience may well not be "whisky buffs" but are more likely to be tourists seeking to experience Scottish culture. The Famous Grouse Experience is as much about the cultural role of the whisky industry as it is about the product itself.

The training and development strategy for The Famous Grouse Experience

The modern tourist is highly sophisticated and the competition for his or her dollars, pounds, euro, yen etc. is fierce. Repeat business and the passing on of good experiences to friends, relatives and colleagues is very important to visitor attractions in Scotland. Sophisticated customers need highly trained staff to provide a memorable experience. Alongside the planning and building of The Famous Grouse Experience was a training and development strategy entitled "Passport to Success" – the name building on the tourism theme.

The core program was intended to be completed before the opening of The Famous Grouse Experience in 2002 and thereafter for all new hires. In addition to the core program there is also a personal development section that is ongoing.

The Passport to Success is divided into six destinations that the individual must "visit," plus the personal development section. The destinations are those that an individual working in The Famous Grouse Experience needs to be competent in. It should be noted that the destinations are not all whisky-related but also include local knowledge.

The destinations are:

» **The Famous Grouse Immersion**: This destination deals with the techniques for whisky production and the Famous Grouse brand itself.
» **Heritage**: The history of Glenturret, the Gloag family and The Edrington Group plus the history of the town of Crieff.
» **Walk the talk**: Training in the guided tour offered to the visitor with details of how to interact with the visitors.
» **Assess your nose and tasting**: Staff need to be able to understand the importance of smell and taste so that they can inform visitors of the "sensual" aspects of the product.
» **Delivering the experience**: Customer care training delivered by external consultants.
» **Out and about**: Information about the red grouse itself plus details of other distilleries and whiskies in the group.
» **Personal Development**: The agreed personal development plan for the individual.

The overall strategy of The Famous Grouse Experience is to provide the most enjoyable and informative way of learning about whisky (and the Famous Grouse brand in particular) and its importance to the culture and economy of Scotland. By including much more than just product knowledge within the training and development strategy it can be seen how that strategy is nested within and supportive of the overall strategy.

By commencing training and development in advance of the attraction's opening it was ensured that the staff were ready and prepared on day one. This may sound like common sense, but many organizations commence new operations before the staff are fully trained and suffer bad publicity for their lack of foresight. The local and national press comment on The Famous Grouse Experience has been highly positive, as has customer feedback.

The training and development were delivered in-house with the exception of "Delivering the Experience," where an outside consultancy was used.

In order to have their passport "stamped" at passport control there are a series of assessment techniques used according to the area of operation in question. These include multiple-choice questions, peer assessment, quizzes etc. The passport provides an *aide-mémoire* for staff as well as providing motivation through the stamps placed in it. It is also a fun way to train and develop.

The training and development strategy is carefully worked out and meets the C-SMART criteria introduced earlier in this material:

» **Customer-centered**: The knowledge that is imparted is derived from the questions and comments of customers who visit distilleries. The whole purpose of the training and development strategy is to equip staff with the skills necessary in order to provide an excellent service to the customer.
» **Specific**: The passport is divided into specific sections dealing with a particular set of activities.
» **Measurable**: Progress is measured using various means of assessment.
» **Agreed**: Individuals discuss progress with their supervisors and managers. Whilst some of the knowledge is mandatory, the personal development section is derived from performance review meetings.

» **Realistic**: There is nothing "difficult" about the Passport to Success. By dividing it into sections, an individual can achieve a degree of success and then move on.
» **Time bound**: The organization and the individual work to an agreed time scale.

Whilst The Famous Grouse Experience is not a large operation, it is a highly professional one in no little part due to the development of a training and development strategy at the same time as the overall strategy for the operation was being developed.

EDRINGTON, HIGHLAND DISTILLERS AND FAMOUS GROUSE TIMELINE

» **1775**: Glenturret Distillery commences operations.
» **1800**: Matthew Gloag & Son founded.
» **1855**: William A. Robertson begins business in Glasgow.
» **1860**: Robertson & Baxter founded.
» **1885**: The North British Distillery Company Ltd founded.
» **1887**: The Highland Distillers Company founded.
» **1936**: Robertson & Baxter supplies first Cutty Sark blend.
» **1961**: Edrington Holdings Ltd established.
» **1970**: Highland Distillers acquires Matthew Gloag & Son Ltd.
» **1993**: Robertson & Baxter acquires a 50% interest in The North British Distillery.
» **1996**: Robertson & Baxter, Clyde Bonding Company, Lang Brothers Ltd and The Clyde Cooperage Company restructured and renamed The Edrington Group.
» **1999**: The Edrington Group acquires Highland Distillers plc.
» **2002**: The Famous Grouse Experience opens and gains a BAFTA in its first year.

KEY INSIGHTS

» Training and development strategy nested within overall strategy for The Famous Grouse Experience.

> » Training commenced prior to opening.
> » Training and strategy met C-SMART criteria.
> » Training and development strategy articulated using a "Passport to Success."

HONG KONG MTR

At the end of hostilities in 1945 the British Crown Colony of Hong Kong, occupied by the Japanese since December 1942, swiftly regained its status as a major East Asian trade center.

The communist takeover of mainland China meant that the colony had to use its own resources to develop new industries. Thousands of newly arrived Chinese from the mainland provided labor and money for the rapid growth of light manufacturing industry during the 1950s and 1960s. In this period, also, the liberal tax policies of the Hong Kong government attracted foreign investment. The resultant economic boom transformed Hong Kong into one of the wealthiest and most productive areas in Asia.

Relations with the People's Republic of China improved and commercial ties with the Chinese prospered with the initiation in the early 1980s of a number of joint economic ventures. Economic growth continued, with Hong Kong becoming one of the "tiger" economies of Asia.

The British lease on the New Territories – lands actually attached to the mainland – was due to expire in 1997. It was clearly impossible that the New Territories could be returned to China with Britain maintaining the island. Talks between China and Great Britain over Hong Kong's future began in 1982 with a legally binding agreement reached between the countries in September 1984 and signed in Beijing in December. The Sino-British Joint Declaration stipulated that all Hong Kong would revert to Chinese sovereignty in 1997. The territory, which would at that time become known as the Hong Kong Special Administrative Region of China, would be allowed to maintain its own legal, social, and economic systems for at least another 50 years, and civil liberties would be guaranteed. China would assume responsibility for foreign affairs and defense.

After many problems and delicate negotiations, Britain ceremonially handed sovereignty over Hong Kong back to China on June 30, 1997.

The Hong Kong SAR has a population of over 6,189,800. The overall population density is 5753 people per sq. km. (14,915 per sq. mile), making Hong Kong one of the most densely populated regions in the world.

Hong Kong has over 1000 miles of roads and with nearly half a million motor vehicles, Hong Kong has one of the highest vehicle densities in the world. The Region is connected by railway with China and has a subway/mass transit system of about 55 miles. Ferries and hydrofoils link various parts of Hong Kong, which is also served by a major international airport near Kowloon. A new Hong Kong International Airport at Chek Lap Kok, situated off Lantau Island, was designed by the British architect Norman Foster. Opened in 1998, it has been designed to handle over 87 million passengers per year.

The density of population means that an efficient urban transportation system is necessary for the economic well being of Hong Kong. The rapid transit/subway system was started in 1979 under the British administration of Hong Kong. Originally the Mass Transit Railway Corporation, the company was renamed MTR Corporation Limited in May 2000. The Initial Public Offering (IPO) was in October 2000.

With the opening of the Tseung Kwan O Line in 2001, the MTR system comprises a railway network of over 55 miles and with 49 stations. Daily patronage of the system is over 2.2 million passengers, making it one of the most intensively utilized rapid transit systems in the world.

MTR provides 19 hours of passenger service daily from 6 a.m. to 1 a.m. with the entire track and lineside maintenance works during the non-traffic hours in the early morning.

To ensure maximum safety and reliability, trains are operated with automatic control and protection systems which regulate the distance between trains, determine the optimal rates of acceleration and braking as well as the coasting speeds on different sections of the track. The routing and timing of train movements are controlled by signaling computer systems according to scheduled timetables from a new control center at Tsing Yi.

The planning of the service timetable is based on passenger demand, taking into account the morning and evening peaks on normal working days. To meet escalating passenger demands, the Corporation expanded its train fleet from 140 cars in 1979 to 1050 cars in 2002 (including 88 cars for the Airport Express), 84% of which are in service to meet the daily morning peak demand.

The lines operated are:

» Kwun Tong Line (running between Yau Ma Tei and Tiu Keng Leng);
» Tsuen Wan Line (running between Tsuen Wan and Central);
» Island Line (running between Sheung Wan and Chai Wan);
» Tseung Kwan O Line (running between Po Lam and North Point);
» Tung Chung Line (running between Tung Chung and Hong Kong); and
» Airport Express (running between the Airport and Hong Kong).

Personnel

Control and maintenance of the railway is carried out 24 hours a day by three major departments:

» the Operations Department for train service and station operations;
» the Rolling Stock Maintenance Department for maintenance of passenger trains; and
» the Infrastructure Maintenance Department for maintenance of structure, tracks, and other fixed installations along the railway lines.

The Corporation's reputation for training and development is widely recognized. In 2000, MTR received the Best Practice Award in training from *Best Practice Management* magazine, two "Excellence in Practice" citations from the American Society for Training and Development, and the Hong Kong Management Association Award for training excellence in 1991, 1992, 1995 and 1996. The company has established a continuous learning culture in the company in order to enable it to survive in a dynamic business environment.

Staff training and development mainly includes two aspects:

» Management Training and Development; and
» Operations Training.

The company training center at its Kowloon Bay headquarters is equipped with comprehensive multimedia facilities, classrooms, computer-based training system, and an audiovisual and multimedia production center. In addition there is operational and technical training equipment including Driving Cab Simulators, Automatic Fare Collection System and Platform Screen Door.

Management Training and Development

The Management Training and Development team aims to achieve various business objectives through working with line departments as strategic partners and developing a motivated, competent and productive workforce in a cost-effective manner.

» **Management development training courses**: A full range of courses have been designed and conducted regularly for different groups of staff to improve their skills and knowledge in tasks and people management. The courses cover a wide range of topics including language, project management, change management, presentation, creativity, and leadership.
» **Value creation seminars**: This is a series of seminars aimed at encouraging employees to face adversities positively and to promote continuous improvement within themselves.
» **Learn-at-lunch (spare)-time**: These sessions are to encourage staff members to make good use of their lunch and spare time by learning new skills. It is perhaps part of the Chinese philosophy and culture that such sessions are highly valued. The employees see that the organization is prepared to invest in them and they in turn are willing to invest some of their personal time.
» **Learning Resource Center**: The Learning Resource Center provides up-to-date facilities and resources for employees to enhance themselves by pursuing knowledge and skills through a variety of self-learning materials.
» **Accelerated Development Program**: As part of management development, the Accelerated Development Program is designed to develop managers and staff at senior supervisory/professional grades with critical skills required by the company in the future. Variants of this program include:

> » Executive Accelerated Development Program.
> » Manager Accelerated Development Program.
> » Professional Development Program.

The objectives of the program are to strengthen participants' business knowledge and management skills as well as sharpen their managerial competencies that are required for future new business operations and challenges ahead.

Participants are recruited into the program through a rigorous selection process. They undergo a 12-month intensive development program with emphasis on both action learning and classroom training. They may be rotated to other positions that are of different grades for a period to broaden their knowledge base and exposure in different functional or cross-functional areas. In this respect there is a similarity with the philosophy being operated at Kodak.

Operations Training

The Operations Training Department is tasked to provide high quality operations, safety and ICT training services in line with the company's business objectives.

A wide range of functional training in technical and operations skills is provided. The training uses the latest training methodology and technique in order to ensure that all staff members are competent at their work, and that their potentials are developed.

> » **Technical training**: This includes basic technical skills and in-depth functional training on Rolling Stock, Automatic Fare Collection, Computer Controlled System, Signaling and Telecommunications, Building Services, Power Distribution, Civil Works and Permanent Way.
> » **Operations and health and safety training**: Operations, safety and refresher training for railway staff.
> » **Information and communication technology (ICT)/multimedia training**: ICT training that is aligned with the Corporation's IT strategy is provided. There is also computer-based training which staff can access at their own time and audiovisual production for corporate training and communications programs.

» **Training consultancy**: The department also provides railway training consultancy services to other overseas railways as and when required. In this respect the department contributes to the income generation of the company.

Graduate Trainee Scheme

For more than two decades MTR has been recruiting graduates from local and overseas universities in different disciplines for succession planning of high-caliber managers and professionals to cope with challenges in a rapidly changing environment.

The Graduate Trainee Scheme provides an opportunity for high caliber graduates to gain an all-round exposure in various functional disciplines through job attachment and on-the-job training. Opportunities and support for training and self-development are available to ensure their continuous professional development.

The Graduate Trainee Scheme covers three main areas.

Graduate engineer

Graduate engineers are given a training program of three to four years that combines theoretical and practical aspects. They work in different engineering departments to gain hands-on experience in areas such as design, installation, commissioning, project management, and maintenance. Experienced managers/engineers who are Chartered Engineers act as mentors to support trainees' development into professional engineers.

MTR has strong links with the Hong Kong Institute of Engineers (HKIE) and the Institution of Electrical Engineers (IEE) in the UK due to the years that Hong Kong spent as a Crown Colony.

Management trainee

Management trainees are provided with a three-year training program with all-round exposure in a particular business discipline through attachments and project-based assignments.

In-house and external training courses, together with guidance by senior managers as mentors, are used to develop and enhance trainees' skills and knowledge in their specialized areas.

The training is designed to develop the trainees into all-round professionals in areas such as Human Resource Management, Property Management, Finance, Marketing, Information Technology, etc.

Railway officer trainee

A railway officer trainee receives a two-year training program in all aspects of running a railway including train operation, depot and station supervision, train service regulation, and the use of control equipment. The trainee is given exposure to the various operational functions in order to attain a concrete foundation in the operations of MTR systems.

Apprentice schemes

The training program for apprentices comprises an all-round basic skill training, directed-objective on-the-job training, and subsequently specialized training in one of the following areas:

» rolling stock maintenance
» infrastructure maintenance
» station-based maintenance
» property management.

Experienced staff act as mentors to pass on their knowledge and experience to the apprentices.

MTR's training and development strategy is one that is well able to support the overall strategy of providing an effective public transport alternative to motor vehicles in a highly congested piece of the world's real estate.

MTR TIMELINE

» **1975**: Mass Transit Railway Corporation founded.
» **1979**: Subway opened – 140 cars owned.
» **1997**: Hong Kong reverts to Chinese control.
» **1997**: New airport opened.

» **2000**: MTR Corporation Ltd formed in May, IPO October. MTR receives the Best Practice Award in training from *Best Practice Management* magazine and two "Excellence in Practice" citations from the American Society for Training and Development.
» **2001**: Tseung Kwan O Line opened.
» **2002**: 1050 cars owned.

KEY INSIGHTS

» Investment at various staff levels.
» Use of apprenticeship schemes to pass on knowledge and expertise.
» Job rotation used as an integral part of training and development.
» Mentors allocated to trainees.

Key Concepts and Thinkers

A glossary of the key terms and concepts of training and development strategy plus details of the key thinkers in the field.

GLOSSARY

Action learning – A system for adult development where the learner(s) take responsibility for the learning process producing their own syllabus etc.

CAL (Computer Assisted Learning) – The use of a computer to train people in tasks using simulations, questioning etc.

CBT (Computer Based Training) – Similar to CAL but with a wider, more developmental focus.

C-SMART – The criteria for writing objectives. C-SMART stands for: Customer-centered, Specific, Measurable, Agreed, Realistic, Time bound.

Coaching – The process in which a more experienced person works on a one-to-one basis with a less experienced person to improve the latter's performance.

CPD (Continuous Professional Development) – The requirement that many professions and jobs have for ongoing training and development to enable the individual to work with new technologies and systems. The standards and requirements are often laid down by professional bodies rather than the employing organization.

Competencies – A set of agreed standards that detail tasks a person should be able to undertake, the range of situations to which they apply and the knowledge and understanding that relates to them.

Core competencies – Those skills that represent the fundamental expertise within the organization.

Cost–benefit analysis – Standard business decision-making tool used to investigate the desirability of an activity or project by comparing the costs likely to be incurred with the benefits that will accrue using a financial basis.

Culture – The values, attitudes, and beliefs ascribed to and accepted by a group, nation, or organization. In effect, ''the way we do things around here.''

Development – A process in which learning occurs through experience and where the results of the learning enhance not only the task skills of the individual, but also his or her attitudes.

Education - The broadening of the knowledge and skills base of the individual and indeed the group with the objective of the individual functioning in and being a benefit to the society he or she lives in.

E-learning - The delivery of learning packages using linked computers.

Empowerment - The process of releasing the full potential of employees in order for them to take on greater responsibility and authority in the decision-making process and providing the resources for this process to occur.

EPD - Kodak's Employee Development Plan drawn up between the individual and his or her line manager.

Human/intellectual capital - The asset value of the knowledge and experience of the employees of an organization.

HRM - Human Resource Management. The term has replaced terms such as personnel management and staffing in order to emphasize the wider issues that are involved with the recruitment, motivation, training, development, and retention of employees.

Infoimaging - The combination of imaging science - cameras, scanners, etc. - with ICT.

Information and Communication Technology (ICT) - Technology related to the connection of computer and communications technology to produce a synergy (see below) between them. ICT was originally known as IT (Information Technology). However more and more computer type applications also involve communication with other computers or communication devices, hence the adoption of the acronym ICT.

iPSS - A web-based integrated Performance Support System devised by SofTools to enable business teams to consistently apply best-practice methods, such as business planning, risk management, or critical decision-making.

Intangible assets - Assets that cannot be touched or seen, but are nevertheless valuable, such as the knowledge base of an organization.

Learning - The process by which behavior and attitudes are changed.

Learning curve - The improvement in performance of a task over time.

Learning cycle – The learning cycle is a four-stage model consisting of: experiencing, evaluating, conceptualizing, and experimenting.

Learning organization – An organization that displays skill in creating, acquiring, and transferring knowledge, and at modifying its behavior to reflect new knowledge and insights.

Learning styles – A person's dominant learning style determines the point at which he or she enters the learning cycle (above). There are four styles: activists, reflectors, theorists, and pragmatists.

Mentoring – The process where an experienced person other than the individual's manager provides counsel and guidance to assist the individual in his or her organizational growth.

Skills gap – The gap between the skills a person has and the skills that he or she needs to carry out a task.

Strategy – The direction and scope of an organization over the long term: ideally which matches its resources to its changing environment, and in particular its markets, customers, or clients so as to meet stakeholder expectations.

Synergy – A phenomenon where the sum of the parts is greater than the whole. A computer and a camera connected to a telephone can aid communication far more than might be expected by examining the individual capabilities of the three components.

Telecottage – A central point, usually in a remote area, that is equipped with ICT facilities and which acts as a base for a group of home workers or trainees.

Training – Specific instruction concerned with the mastering of a particular task or set of tasks.

Training and development strategy – The direction and scope of the training and development opportunities developed and provided by the organization for its employees and other concerned partners: ideally which matches the training and development provided to both the needs of the organization and the individual in order to ensure that the organization can respond to changes in its external environment.

Training cycle – The process of the identification of training needs, the implementation of training, the evaluation of the training, and any further training needs that become apparent in line with the organization's training policies.

Training Needs Analysis (TNA) - A systematic review of the current skills base against organizational requirements in order to identify the skills gap.

KEY THINKERS

All of the books referred to in this section are listed fully in Chapter 9. In addition to the thinkers listed below many of the "gurus" of management such as Tom Peters, Rosabeth Moss Kanter, Charles Handy and John Harvey Jones have stressed the importance of training and development to business growth and survival.

Boydell, Tom

Prior to establishing his own companies in the field of training and development, Tom Boydell was for 20 years an academic at Sheffield Hallam University in the UK. Much of his work has been in the effective identification of training needs within organizations. Like many other writers in the training and development field, Boydell stresses the importance of both individual and team training and development. He is also concerned to ensure that the success of training and development programs are assessed using objective criteria so the "investment" can be transparent and training and development not seen as a cost that has little payback.

Books

» *Experiential Learning* (1976).
» *Self-Development* (with Mike Pedler) (1979).
» *Managing Yourself* (with Mike Pedler) (1986).
» *Management Self-Development* (1989).
» *A Guide to the Identification of Training Needs* (1990).
» *Learning Company* (1991).
» *Towards the Learning Company* (with Mike Pedler and John Burgoyne) (1994).
» *Identifying Training Needs* (with Malcolm Leary) (1996).
» *A Manager's Guide to Self-Development* (with John Burgoyne and Mike Pedler) (2001).

Brelade, Sue

A UK-based human resource consultant, Brelade has gained wide-ranging experience in the practical application of training and development and HR, working in a variety of industry sectors including central and local government, contracting, media, travel, financial services, and with trade bodies. She has worked within the UK and across Europe where her multilingual skills in the design and delivery of human resource solutions have given her a reputation for understanding and meeting business needs. She is the author of a number of published articles in professional journals.

Brelade has stressed the importance of knowledge management as one of the most important management themes of recent years. She has shown how organizations are embracing knowledge management in an attempt to offset the damaging effects of downsizing and to aid greater job mobility. Although the concept of the learning organization owes much to HR, knowledge management tends instead to be treated as an issue for information systems experts, largely bypassing HR. Brelade believes that the challenge for HR professionals is to place knowledge management firmly within an HR framework and to develop the competencies to do so.

Books

» *Financial Times Management Briefings – 101 Tips for Trainers* (with Tony Miller) (1997).
» *Financial Times Management Briefings – Human Resources Practical Training Strategies for the Future* (with Tony Miller and Chris Harman) (1998).
» *Knowledge Management and the Role of HR* (2000).
» *Knowledge Management* (with Chris Harman) (2001).

Ginnodo, William

Bill Ginnodo is the publisher of Pride's Publications, having previously served in a number of large US corporations plus holding the position of Executive Director of the Quality and Productivity Management Association (QPMA). In his work on empowerment Ginnodo has emphasized the concept that training is much more than a remedial activity. He sees empowerment training together with coaching as highly influential in developing empowered employees. Ginnodo has also participated in the President's Executive Exchange Program.

Book
» *The Power of Empowerment* (1997).

Honey, Peter
A highly respected name in training and development, Peter Honey together with Alan Mumford is best known for work on the learning styles linked to the ideas of David Kolb's book. The tests that they have developed to ascertain an individual's preferred learning style and thus his or her optimum point of entry into the learning cycle are used across the globe.

Of Peter Honey's 50+ major publications (a number of which are published by his own publishing company) the most relevant to the topic in this material are listed below:

Books
» *The Manual of Learning Styles* (with Alan Mumford) (1982).
» *The Learning Styles Questionnaire* (with Alan Mumford) (1982).
» *Using Your Learning Styles* (with Alan Mumford) (1986).
» *Face to Face Skills* (1990).

Kirkpatrick, Donald L.
From the 1960s onwards Kirkpatrick has been looking at the evaluation of training and development. He has described a four-stage evaluation model – reaction, learning, behavior, and results.

The simplicity and common sense of Kirkpatrick's model has been criticized as implying that conducting an evaluation is a standardized, prepackaged process.

However, Kirkpatrick does offer some flexibility and has advised trainers to borrow evaluation forms, procedures, designs, approaches, techniques, and methods from other people. He has also encouraged trainers to understand the difference between proof and evidence of training results. Kirkpatrick himself points out the complications;

especially soft-skills training and development, as there are too many variables that can impact performance, other than the training itself.

Books

» *How to Train and Develop Supervisors* (1993).
» *Evaluating Training Programs* (1996).

Kline, Peter

Peter Kline, based in South Bend, IN, has pioneered methods of accelerated learning that have been used both by trainers and schoolteachers. Together with Bernard Saunders, Kline has produced *Ten Steps to a Learning Organization* – a practical guide that can be contextualized to fit specific organizational needs.

Kline has been a promoter of innovative learning methods and in addition to his non-fiction works is also an accomplished fiction writer.

Books

» *School Success – the Inside Story* (1992).
» *Why America's Children Can't Think* (2002).
» *Ten Steps to a Learning Organization* (with Bernard Saunders) (1993).

Kolb, David A.

David Kolb is Professor of Organizational Behavior at the Weatheread School of Management. He joined the School in 1976. Born in 1939, Kolb received his higher education at Knox College and Harvard in 1967. Besides his work on experiential learning, Kolb is also known for his contribution to thinking around organizational behavior with interests in the nature of individual and social change, experiential learning, career development, and executive and professional education.

Working with Roger Fry, Kolb created his famous model out of four elements: concrete experience; observation and reflection; the formation of abstract concepts; and testing in new situations. He represented these in the famous experiential learning cycle discussed in Chapter 6 of this material. In his work he has argued that the learning cycle can begin at any one of the four points – and that it should really be approached as a continuous spiral. However, he has suggested that the learning process often begins with a person carrying out a particular action and then seeing the effect of the action in this situation. Following this, the second step is to understand these effects in the particular instance so that if the same action were taken in the same circumstances it would be possible to anticipate what would follow from the action. In this pattern the third step would be understanding the general principle under which the particular instance falls.

Books

» *Organizational Psychology* (1974).
» *Changing Human Behavior* (with Ralph K. Schwitzgebel) (1974).
» *Organizational Behavior* 6th edn (with Joyce S. Osland and Irwin M. Rubin) (1991).
» *The Organizational Behavior Reader* 6th edn (with Joyce S. Osland and Irwin M. Rubin) (1995).

Logan, David

A professor at the University of Southern California, Logan together with ex-athlete John King is a keen advocate of coaching as a component of empowerment.

Logan comments that there is nothing new about coaching. Its basic concepts have been around since human beings began competing in athletic contests etc. Athletes, especially, have used coaches to guide them through the process of transforming their potential into top performance. Logan points out that business managers face a similar problem i.e. getting maximum performance out of their employees. Logan believes that the payoff for becoming a manager-coach is clear: manager-coaches are more productive, their workplaces are more efficient, their people constantly develop their skills, and their companies' performances improve.

Book

» *The Coaching Revolution* (with John King) (2001).

Mayo, Andrew

Originally a chemistry graduate, Andrew Mayo is an international consultant in human resource management and organizational development. Much of his work is involved with ensuring that the training and development process meets the needs both of the organization and the trainee.

Mayo spent 30 years working for major international companies (he was the Director of Human Resource Development at International Computers Limited – ICL) and so is able to blend practice and theory.

Mayo is especially interested in the value of intellectual capital and how this can be developed with an approach to training and development that balances organizational and individual needs.

Books

» *Managing Careers* (1991).
» *The Power of Learning* (with Elizabeth Lank) (1994).
» *Motivating People in Lean Organizations* (with Linda Holbeche) (1997).
» *Creating a Training and Development Strategy* (1998).
» *Managing Career Development* (1999).
» *Human Value of Enterprise: Valuing People as Assets* (2001).

Miller, Tony

Tony Miller is the Managing Director of Management Performance Solutions Ltd, a company that specializes in creating added value solutions. His experience in HR has enabled him to work at strategic level with government, national committees, on EU projects, and with blue-chip companies worldwide. He has appeared on television and in a number of documentaries, and directed the EU video *Model for European Business Success*. He is the author of numerous published articles in professional journals and joint author of three professional psychology reports on productivity improvements.

Miller has worked in most EU countries, Pakistan, the Middle East and Australia, and the USA.

Miller has considered how training and development can not only meet the strategic needs of the organization, but can also deliver measurable value. He suggests that to do this management must:

» identify the need for change;
» assess their department's current position and skill-set;
» understand the information requirements of internal customers;
» identify the skills required to deliver measurable value;
» understand the strategy process and the implications for HR; and
» establish credibility with key figures in the organization.

Books

» *Financial Times Management Briefings – 101 Tips for Trainers* (with Sue Brelade) (1997).
» *Strategies for the Future* (with Sue Brelade and Chris Harman) (1998).
» *Redesigning HR for Strategic Advantage* (1999).
» *Financial Times Management Briefings – Human Resources Practical Training* (1997).

Pettinger, Richard

Richard Pettinger is a UK-based writer of a large number of HR and general management books in addition to his work as an academic at University College, London. Pettinger has been an advocate of training and development as an investment to be made rather than as a cost to be borne. He has had considerable experience of working on the implementation of training and development programs with a variety of organizations both in the UK and throughout Europe.

He has also commented on the changing nature of the workforce and in *Managing the Flexible Workforce* (1998) he has shown how important training and development are to the management of a workforce that is now far more flexible both in terms of location, times of work, skills, and contractual arrangements. Such flexibility, he argues, requires a mutual responsibility from both the individual and the organization if the human resource is to be used to maximum advantage.

His books with relevance to training and development are listed below.

Books

» *Introduction to Corporate Strategy* (1996).
» *Managing the Flexible Workforce* (1998).
» *Effective Employee Relations* (1999).
» *Mastering Organizational Behavior* (2000).
» *Mastering Employee Development* (2002).
» ExpressExec *Global Organizations* (2002).
» ExpressExec *Managing the Flexible Workforce* (2002).
» ExpressExec *The Learning Organization* (2002).

Saunders, Bernard

Bernard Saunders worked with Peter Kline (above) on *Ten Steps to a Learning Organization.* Like Kline, Saunders has been involved with innovative methods of training and development working with many Fortune 500 companies consulting in the areas of organizational change.

Book

» *Ten Steps to a Learning Organization* (with Peter Kline) (1993).

Shea-Schultz, Heather

Heather Shea-Schultz has worked with Tom Peters as well as being a VP for Learn2.

She has shown a particular interest in the use of the Internet as a medium for training and development. She has demonstrated how properly designed Web-based training and development programs can save both time and money without any sacrifice of effectiveness. She stresses, however, that great care needs to be taken with program design and that technophobia may need to be overcome before individuals can benefit from online training and development.

Book

» *Online Learning Today* (with John Fogarty) (2002).

Stewart, Jim

Working at the University of Nottingham in the UK, Stewart is an organizational and management development specialist who sees training and development as essential components in the change process within organizations. He demonstrates how learning organizations find that implanting change can be less of a threat to those involved due to the fact that individuals know they will be given the training and development needed to perform new tasks and roles. He has also stressed the importance of team training and development alongside that of the individual.

Books

» *Managing Change through Training and Development* (1991).
» *Speedtraining* (1993).

Tulgan, Bruce

Bruce Tulgan is internationally recognized as the leading expert on young people in the workplace. He is an advisor to business leaders all over the world and the author of 12 different books and numerous management-training programs.

Since 1995, Tulgan has addressed tens of thousands of leaders and managers in hundreds of organizations ranging from JP Morgan to JC Penney. He has been called "the new Tom Peters" by many who have seen him speak, and was named by *Management Today* in the UK as one of the few contemporary figures to stand out as a "management guru."

His writings have appeared in numerous magazines and newspapers, including the *Harvard Business Review, Business Week*, the *New York Times*, the *Los Angeles Times*, and *USA Today*.

Before founding his company, Rainmaker Thinking, in 1993, he practiced law at the Wall Street firm of Carter, Ledyard & Milburn. He graduated with high honors from Amherst College, received his law degree from the New York University School of Law, and is still a member of the Bar in Massachusetts and New York.

He is considered an expert on the behavior of Generation X and the methods organizations can use to maximize the talent within their staff base. His most relevant books to the topic of training and development strategies are listed below.

Books

» *Managing Generation X* (1996).
» *The Manager's Pocket Guide to Generation X* (1997).
» *Work This Way* (1998).
» *Managing Generation X: How to Bring Out the Best in Young People* (2000).
» *Winning the Talent Wars* (2001).

Resources for Implementing a Training and Development Strategy

This chapter is concerned with where to find resources for the study of the development and implementation of a training and development strategy:

- » books;
- » journals; and
- » Websites.

BOOKS

(Note: Dates of books in this chapter may differ from those shown in previous chapters. The dates shown here are of the latest editions whereas those in the chapter material are the dates of first publication.)

Boydell, T. (1976), *Experiential Learning*. University of Manchester, Manchester.

Boydell, T. & Pedler, M. (eds) (1979), *Self-Development*. MCB, Bradford.

Boydell, T. (1989), *Management Self-Development*. International Labor Organization, Geneva.

Boydell, T. (1990), *A Guide to the Identification of Training Needs*. Chartered Institute of Personnel and Development, London.

Boydell, T. & Leary, M. (1996), *Identifying Training Needs*. Chartered Institute of Personnel and Development, London.

Boydell, T., Burgoyne, J., & Pedler, M. (1996), *Towards the Learning Company*. McGraw-Hill, London.

Boydell, T. & Pedler, M. (1999), *Managing Yourself*. Lemos & Crane, London.

Boydell, T., Burgoyne, J., & Pedler, M. (2001), *A Manager's Guide to Self-Development*. McGraw-Hill, London.

Brelade, S., & Miller A. (1997), *Financial Times Management Briefings – 101 Tips for Trainers*. Financial Times/Prentice Hall, London.

Brelade S., Miller A., & Harman, C. (1997), *Financial Times Management Briefings – Human Resources Practical Training Strategies for the Future*. Financial Times/Prentice Hall, London.

Brelade, S. (2000), *Knowledge Management and the Role of HR*. Financial Times/Prentice Hall, London.

Brelade, S. & Harman C. (2001), *Knowledge Management*. Hawksmere, London.

Cartwright, R. (1999), *Mastering Customer Relations*. Macmillan, Basingstoke.

Cartwright, R. (2001), *Managing Diversity*. Capstone, Oxford.

Cartwright, R. (2003), *Training and Development Express*. Capstone, Oxford.

Garvin, D.A. (1993), "Building a Learning Organization." *Harvard Business Review*, July/August (1993).

Ginnodo, W. (1997), *The Power of Empowerment*. Pride Publications, Arlington Heights, IL.

Harris, P.R. & Moran, R.T. (2000), *Managing Cultural Differences*. Gulf Publishing Co, Houston.

Herzberg, F. (1962), *Work and the Nature of Man*. World Publishing, New York.

Honey, P. (1990), *Face to Face Skills*. Gower, London.

Honey, P. & Mumford, A. (1982), *The Manual of Learning Styles*. P. Honey, Maidenhead.

Honey, P. & Mumford, A. (1982), *The Learning Styles Questionnaire*. P. Honey, Maidenhead.

Honey, P. & Mumford, A. (1986), *Using Your Learning Styles*. P. Honey, Maidenhead.

Johnson, G. & Scholes, K. (1984), *Exploring Corporate Strategy*. Prentice Hall, London.

Joynt, P. & Morton, R. (eds) (1999), *The Global HR Manager*. Chartered Institute of Personnel and Development, London.

King, D.S. (1987), *The New Right*. Macmillan, Basingstoke.

Kirkpatrick, D.L. (1993), *How to Train and Develop Supervisors*. Amacom, New York.

Kirkpatrick, D.L. (1998), *Evaluating Training Programs*. Pfeiffer Wiley, New York.

Kline, P. (1992), *School Success – The Inside Story*. Great Ocean Publishing, Arlington, VA.

Kline, P. (2002), *Why America's Children Can't Think*. Inner Ocean Publishing, Alexander, NC.

Kline, P. & Saunders, B. (1993), *Ten Steps to a Learning Organization*. Great Ocean Publishing, Arlington, VA.

Kolb, D.A. (1974). *Organizational Psychology*. Prentice Hall, New York.

Kolb, D.A. & Schwitzgebel, R.K., (1974) *Changing Human Behavior*. Prentice Hall, New York.

Kolb, D.A., Osland, S., & Rubin, Irwin M. (1991), *Organizational Behavior*, 6th edn Prentice Hall, New York.

Kolb, D.A., Osland, S., & Rubin, Irwin M. (1995), *The Organizational Behavior Reader*, 6th edn Prentice Hall, New York.

Kouzes, J. & Posner, B.Z. (1987), *The Leadership Challenge*. Jossey-Bass, San Francisco.

Kouzes, J. & Posner, B.Z. (1995), *Credibility*. Jossey-Bass, San Francisco.

Lessem, R. (1990), *Developmental Management*. Blackwell, Oxford.

Lewis, R.D. (1996), *When Cultures Collide*. Nicholas Brealey, London.

Lynn, J. & Jay, A. (1989). *The Complete Yes Prime Minister*, BBC Books, London.

Logan, D. & King, J. (2001). *The Coaching Revolution*. Adams Media Corporation, Holbrook, MA.

Mayo, A. (1991), *Managing Careers*. Chartered Institute of Personnel and Development, London.

Mayo, A. & Lank, E. (1994), *The Power of Learning*. Chartered Institute of Personnel and Development, London.

Mayo, A. & Holbeche, L. (1997), *Motivating People in Lean Organizations*. Butterworth-Heinemann, Oxford.

Mayo, A. (1998), *Creating a Training and Development Strategy*. Chartered Institute of Personnel and Development, London.

Mayo, A. (1999), *Managing Career Development*. Fenman Training, London.

Mayo, A. (2001), *Human Value of Enterprise: Valuing People as Assets*. Nicholas Brealey, London.

Miller, A. (1999), *Redesigning HR for Strategic Advantage*. Prentice Hall, London.

Murrell, K.L. & Meredith, M. (2000), *Empowering Employees*. McGraw-Hill, New York.

Pettinger, R. (1996), *Introduction to Corporate Strategy*. Palgrave-Macmillan, Basingstoke.

Pettinger, R. (1998), *Managing the Flexible Workforce*. Cassel, London.

Pettinger, R. (1999), *Effective Employee Relations*. Kogan Page, London.

Pettinger, R. (2002), *ExpressExec Global Organizations*. Capstone, Oxford.

Pettinger, R. (2002), *ExpressExec Managing the Flexible Workforce*. Capstone, Oxford.

Pettinger, R. (2002), *ExpressExec The Learning Organization*. Capstone, Oxford.

Pettinger, R. (2002), *Mastering Employee Development*. Palgrave Macmillan, Basingstoke.

Shea-Schultz, H. & Fogarty, J. (2002), *Online Learning Today*. Berrett-Koehler, San Francisco.

Stewart, J. (1991), *Managing Change through Training and Development*. Kogan Page, London.

Thomson, R. (1959), *The Psychology of Thinking*. Penguin, London.

Trompenaars, F. (1993), *Riding the Waves of Culture*. Economist Books, London.

Tulgan, B. (1996), *Managing Generation X*. Capstone, Oxford.

Tulgan, B. (1997), *The Manager's Pocket Guide to Generation X*. HRD Press, Amherst, MA.

Tulgan, B. (1998), *Work This Way*. Capstone, Oxford.

Tulgan, B. (2000) *Managing Generation X: How to Bring Out the Best in Young People*. W. Norton, New York.

Tulgan, B. (2001). *Winning the Talent Wars*. Nicholas Brealey, Naperville, IL.

Ward, G.C., Burns, R., & Burns, K. (1990), *The Civil War*. Alfred A. Knopf, New York.

Yip, G.S. (1992), *Total Global Strategy*, Prentice Hall, Eaglewood Cliffs, NJ.

FOR FURTHER INFORMATION ABOUT THE FAMOUS GROUSE AND SCOTCH WHISKY

Hills, P. (2000), *Appreciating Whisky*. Collins, London.

Hughes, J. (2002), *Scotland's Malt Whisky Distilleries: Survival of the Fittest*. Tempus, Gloucester, UK.

FOR FURTHER INFORMATION ABOUT KODAK

Brayer, E. (1996), *George Eastman: A Biography*. Johns Hopkins University, Baltimore.

Kodak (1990), *A Journey into 75 years of Kodak Research*. Kodak, Rochester, NY.

Mitchell, B. & Hosking Smith, J. (1998), *Click - A Story about George Eastman*. Carolrhoda Books, Minneapolis, MN.

Swasy, A. (1997), *Changing Focus: Kodak and the Battle to Save a Great American Company*. Time Books, New York.

JOURNALS AND PROFESSIONAL ORGANIZATIONS

The American Management Association (AMA)

The world's leading membership-based management development organization. AMA offers a full range of business education and management development programs for individuals and organizations in Europe, the Americas, and Asia. Through a variety of seminars and conferences, assessments and customized learning solutions, books and online resources, more than 700,000 AMA members and customers a year learn superior business skills and best management practices from a faculty of top practitioners. The online facilities offer access to a wide range of articles including issues related to training and development.
www.amanet.org

American Society for Training and Development (ASTD)

Based in Alexandria, VA, the ASTD produces *T&D* Magazine, a monthly online magazine that covers a wide range of training and development issues. The ASTD also publishes books on training and development and has developed related software.
www.astd.org

Career Development International

A UK-based journal that provides an international forum for all those who wish to gain a greater understanding of career development and its associated issues. It forms an arena for academics to share information and ideas that will help them examine the links between individual career progression and organizational needs.
www.emeraldinsight.com/cdi.htm

Harvard Business Review

Leading business and management resource. Read worldwide and features contributions by the leading names in business and management. Published 10 times p.a. and available by subscription.
www.hbsp.harvard.edu/products/hbr

Human Resource Development Quarterly (HRDQ)

A journal published by Wiley in the US and focusing directly on the evolving field of human resource development (HRD). The journal has become a major forum for interdisciplinary exchange on the subject of HRD and issues related to training and development.
http://www.interscience.wiley.com/jpages/1044-8004/

Human Resource Management International Digest

A digest of useful HR articles from many sources gathered on a global basis and published seven times p.a. Available on subscription.
www.mcb.co.uk/hrmid/html

HR Magazine

An HR magazine covering a wide range of issues including training and development. Published by the Society for Human Resource Management in Alexandria, VA.
www.shrm.org

Industry and Higher Education

Published six times per year in the US, this journal is dedicated to the relationships between business and industry and higher education institutions. With a strong emphasis on practical aspects, the journal covers organizational, economic, political, legal, and social issues relating to developments in education-industry collaboration. The links between organizations and academic institutions make this a useful journal for those involved in training and development strategy as shown by the key topics listed below:

» Technology transfer from research to commercial application
» Preparing students for the world of work

- » International and national initiatives for collaboration
- » Respective needs in the industry–education relationship
- » Lifelong learning
- » Funding of higher education
- » Educating for entrepreneurship
- » University–industry training programs
- » Business–education partnerships for social and economic progress
- » Skills needs and the role of higher education
- » Formation, structure and performance of academic spin-off companies
- » Academic accreditation for workplace learning
- » Personnel exchange
- » Industrial liaison in universities
- » Intellectual property in the HE sector
- » Distance education.

http://www.ippublishing.com/general_industry.asp

International Journal of Human Resource Management

A journal that is concerned with strategic human resource management and future trends in a global environment. Published eight times p.a. by Routledge and available on subscription.
www.tandf.co.uk/journals/routledge

The International Journal of Training and Development

This journal provides an international forum for the reporting of high-quality research, analysis and debate for the benefit of the academic and corporate communities, as well as those engaged in public policy formulation and implementation.

Multidisciplinary, international and comparative, the journal publishes research which ranges from the theoretical, conceptual, and methodological to more policy-oriented types of work. The journal reports on academic work which specifies and tests the explanatory variables which may be related to training.
http://www.blackwellpublishers.co.uk/asp/journal.asp?ref=1360-3736&src=sub

International Personnel Management Association (IPMA)

Headquartered in Alexandria, VA, the IPMA is a non-profit organization representing the interests of public sector HR professionals.

The objectives of the IPMA are:

» to promote excellence through ongoing development of both professional and personal career development;
» to enhance the image of HR professionals by recognizing their contributions to public service;
» to foster fairness and equity by promoting application of merit principles and equal opportunity; and
» to promote communication and sharing of information among human resource professionals.

IPMA members are key executives, managers, supervisors, and related professionals responsible for a variety of HR functions for federal, state, and local governments around the USA and the world.

The IPMA offers the following publications to its members and subscribers:

» *IPMA News*: Monthly.
» *Public Personnel Management* (*PPM*): Quarterly.
» *HR Bulletin*: Weekly by e-mail.
» *International News*: Bimonthly newsletter for both members and non-members that features HR news from around the world.
» *Federal Section*: Bimonthly newsletter e-mailed to all Federal Section members encompassing federal and personnel issues.
» *Assessment Council News* (*ACN*): Serves as a source of information about significant activities of the council, a medium of dialogue and information exchange among members, a method for dissemination of research findings, and a forum for the publication of letters and articles of general interest.

www.ipma-hr.org

The Journal of Career Development

Published by Kluwer Academic in New York, the Journal of Career Development provides the professional, the public, and policymakers with the latest in career development theory, research, and practice, while focusing on the impact of theory and research on practice. Among the topics covered are career education, adult career development, career development of special needs populations, and career and leisure.

http://www.kluweronline.com/issn/0894-8453

The Journal of Management Development

Produced 10 times a year, the journal explores the concepts, models, tools and processes which companies are using to help their managers become better equipped to tackle the challenges and opportunities of change.

Coverage includes:

» Competence-based management development
» Developing leadership skills
» Developing women in management
» Global management
» The new technology of management development
» Team building
» Organizational development and change
» Performance appraisal.

www.emeraldinsight.com/jmd.htm

People Management

Magazine of the UK Chartered Institute of Personnel and Development (CIPD). Contains articles on all aspects of personnel and training with especial relevance to the UK. Available by subscription and published every two weeks.

The CIPD is the publisher of a large number of HR-related books.

www.peoplemanagement.co.uk

The Training Journal

A UK-based monthly journal that was originally founded as *The Training Officer* in 1965 and was the official publication of the Institute of Training Officers.

The journal's philosophy: to deliver informative, timely and practical content of the highest quality to assist anyone involved in workplace learning, training, and development.

www.trainingjournal.co.uk

Training magazine

A 37-year-old professional development magazine, published in Minneapolis, that advocates training and workforce development as a business tool. The magazine delves into management issues such as leadership and succession planning, HR issues such as recruitment and retention, and training issues such as learning theory, on-the-job skills assessments, and aligning core workforce competencies to enhance the bottom line impact of training and development programs. Written for training, human resources and business management professionals in all industries.

Editorials include best practice case studies for a wide range of business challenges, investigative analyses of training's strategic applications within leading global organizations, and in-depth research.

www.trainingsupersite.com/training

WEBSITES

» www.amanet.org: American Management Association Website.
» www.astd.org: American Society for Training and Development Website.
» www.edringtongroup.com: The Edrington Group Website.
» www.famousgrouse.com: Famous Grouse Website.
» www.inst-mgt.org.uk: Institute of Management (UK) Website.
» www.kodak.com: Kodak Website.
» www.mtrcorp.com: Hong Kong MTR Website.
» www.open.ac.uk: Open University Website.
» www.therobertsontrust.org.uk: The Robertson Trust Website.
» www.scotch-whisky.org.uk: Scotch Whisky Association Website.

» www.tripfp.com: Tricon International Restaurants Inc Website.
» www.uhi.ac.uk: University of the Highlands and Islands Millennium Institute Website.
» www.whisky-heritage.co.uk: Scottish Whisky Heritage Centre Website.
» www.yum.com: Yum Brands Website.

For information about ExpressExec and SofTools

» www.expressexec.com: ExpressExec Website.
» www.SofTools.net: SofTools Website.

Ten Steps to Implementing a Training and Development Strategy

This chapter contains 10 steps to the implementation of a training and development strategy:

1 Know and understand the vision and goals of the organization.
2 Ensure that the training and development strategy is nested within the overall strategy of the organization.
3 Assess the current skills base of the organization.
4 Predict the skills that the organization will need in the future based on an analysis of the external environment.
5 Decide how the gap between current and future skills will be bridged.
6 Set success criteria for the strategy.
7 Ensure that there are adequate resources for the strategy.

8 Ensure that the strategy does not cause a culture conflict within parts of the organization.

9 Carry out a cost-benefit analysis.

10 Gain agreement for the strategy from all stakeholders.

1. KNOW AND UNDERSTAND THE VISION AND GOALS OF THE ORGANIZATION

Organizations resource training and development to further the goals of the organization. The individual may well have his or her own personal agenda for undertaking training and development activities and provided these do not conflict with the organizational agenda there should be few problems.

The organizational strategy and goals are the foundation from which all organizational activities including training and development flow. The better the goals are understood, the more individuals can make an informed contribution.

Those responsible for drawing up the organizational strategy need to ensure that the staff are aware of why the particular strategy and goals have been suggested and what their role is in fulfilling them.

2. ENSURE THAT THE TRAINING AND DEVELOPMENT STRATEGY IS NESTED WITHIN THE OVERALL STRATEGY OF THE ORGANIZATION

It should stand to reason that subordinate strategies such as training and development are derived from and are nested in the overall strategy of the organization. Unfortunately there are still training and development programs to be found that do not appear to be derived from the organizational strategy. Such training and development tends to be piecemeal and may contribute little to the organization's effectiveness and efficiency while, at the same time, consuming precious financial and human resources.

It may be that the organization is willing to let individuals learn and develop in areas that are of personal interest. This is permissible when such programs form part of the motivational strategy of the organization. Normally, however, the organization should be able to ask: "What does the organization gain from this training and development in terms of improved performance and new skills as a result of expending resources on the training and development?"

The answer should be one that reflects the skills, etc. that the overall organizational strategy requires in order to be successful.

3. ASSESS THE CURRENT SKILLS BASE OF THE ORGANIZATION

Training and development are undertaken to fill the skills gap that an organization identifies. It is the skills gap that acts as a barrier to carrying out the overall strategy of the organization.

Before the skills gap can be identified, it is necessary to identify the current skills base within the organization.

Organizations should take considerable care in recording the skills of their employees. Such records may be kept by the HR department, the training department if there is one, or even section/department managers.

Skills are gained through courses, programs, coaching sessions, etc. and need to be recorded. There are many managers who will relate how organizations have turned to recruitment or outsourcing in order to make use of a particular skill, only to find that it was present all along in one of their own employees.

Skills acquired outside the workplace should also be noted whenever possible. Performance reviews should include a section where an employee can indicate his or her particular skills. In the late 1980s one UK local authority constructed a database (using what was then very new technology indeed) so that those working on projects could log on and see if there was somebody else in another part of the organization who had this or that particular skill. There was also a protocol worked out that enabled time to be bought from the individual's manager. Such an approach made a much wider and more effective use of the organizational skill base.

Without the necessary skills within the organization or easily accessible to it then the overall strategy is unlikely to be successful. The aim of the training and development strategy should be to ensure that the organization has access to the skills it needs now and in the future in order to achieve its overall goals.

4. PREDICT THE SKILLS THAT THE ORGANIZATION WILL NEED IN THE FUTURE BASED ON AN ANALYSIS OF THE EXTERNAL ENVIRONMENT

Strategies by definition are about the present and the future. They may be informed by the past but they are forward-looking. Those responsible for training and development need to assess the future skills needs of the organization based on the overall organizational strategy and goals and then develop their training and development strategy so that those skills are in place when needed. It is far better to have the skills in place before they are needed – the proactive approach – than to be constantly trying to catch up – a reactive approach. Success tends towards the proactive approach.

Even if the skills can be obtained fairly quickly, the laws of supply and demand suggest that the organization will have to pay a premium to obtain them.

5. DECIDE HOW THE GAP BETWEEN CURRENT AND FUTURE SKILLS WILL BE BRIDGED

The *raison d'être* of a training and development section or department is first to identify the skills gap and then to decide how it is to be bridged. The actual bridging process is tactical, not strategic. The strategic decisions that need to be made relate to the ways in which the resources for training and development are to be used. There are a number of strategies that can be employed and most organizations will employ a number of them. They are:

» training current staff through formal programs;
» using outside providers for training and development;
» employing one's own trainers;
» recruiting new staff;
» coaching and on-the-job training; and
» outsourcing certain operations to those outside the organization who have the skills.

The resources for training and development are usually finite and thus the balance that is made between the different ways of bridging the training gap will be very important.

Using one's own staff for training and coaching may appear to be the cheapest option, but the fact is that whilst they are conducting training etc. their own job and tasks may be suffering.

6. SET SUCCESS CRITERIA FOR THE STRATEGY

Organizations should never enter into any activity before first deciding the success criteria. Unless this is done it is impossible to monitor and evaluate the activity.

Training and development are no different. The tactical training and development plans need success criteria, as does the overall training and development strategy. It is important to state at the beginning that, "This strategy will have been a success if … " The criteria should be written in the C-SMART format (Customer-centered, Specific, Measurable, Realistic, Agreed, and Time bound).

Once the success criteria are in place it becomes possible to evaluate the progress of the strategy in an objective manner. This allows any remedial action to be put into place quickly.

There is nothing wrong with making changes to a strategy either to keep it on track or to respond to changed conditions. The emergent strategy that develops over time nearly always deviates from the planned strategy due to changes in the business environment. When change is necessary, this should be accompanied by a revisiting and amendment of the success criteria.

7. ENSURE THAT THERE ARE ADEQUATE RESOURCES FOR THE STRATEGY

A strategy that is not resourced properly is never going to meet its success criteria. Whist budgeting can never be an exact science, the strategy should have sufficient resources allocated to it to meet predicted changes in the environment and an additional contingency fund.

In addition to monitoring the progress of the strategy, the progress of the use of resources also needs careful monitoring.

It might be thought that it is common sense to ensure that there are adequate resources available to allow the strategy to be successful, but the history of organizational activity is littered with examples of under-resourcing.

One of the main reasons for the under-resourcing of proposed strategies and activities is that it may be easier to "sell" the strategy by suggesting that the actual costs may be much lower than believed.

This can cause considerable problems. In 2002 it was announced that many of the Apache attack helicopters purchased by the UK's Ministry of Defence (*sic*) would have to be put in store as the training of the pilots was running well behind schedule. There is, in fact, little point in having a strategy of an air-mobile attack force unless that strategy also includes the training of pilots before the helicopters are delivered. No commercial airline would spend millions of dollars on a new model unless it was accompanied by simultaneous training of the pilots to fly it. A commercial airline cannot afford to have an investment static on the ground – it needs it in the air, full of passengers, and earning revenue.

8. ENSURE THAT THE STRATEGY DOES NOT CAUSE A CULTURE CONFLICT WITHIN THE ORGANIZATION

Organizations tend to be made up of departments that focus on particular activities – finance, research, sales, training and development etc. Each of these areas of organizational life will have its own strategies nested within the overall organizational strategy.

It is important that each individual strategy adds to the success of the overall strategy. It is sometimes the case that individual parts of the organization will adopt their own strategies that are not in total align-ment with that of the overall strategy. Departments may be tempted to undertake their own training and development strategies – this is acceptable as long as there is no duplication of effort and that what they do is in accordance with the culture of the organization. In their excellent satires, *The Complete Yes Prime Minister* (1989), Jonathan Lynn and Antony Jay have their "hero," the fictional UK Prime Minister Jim Hacker, questioning whether there really need to be separate music schools for the Army, the Royal Navy, the Royal Marines and the Royal Air Force. "Is there," he questions, "a difference between the way a soldier and a sailor play the bassoon?"

Such ambiguities tend to be historical. However, they still occur and the writer well remembers working with an organization not many years ago and discovering that the IT from one department could not "speak" to that from another due to the fact that different, incompatible software packages were being used – a situation that also included different training programs. Not only was communication made less efficient but also the costs of providing two types of training were higher than those that would have been incurred had only one system been in place. The reasons were irrational but historic. One department had adopted computers much earlier than the other and unfortunately the computerization of the organization had occurred piecemeal rather than in a planned manner. It was also unfortunate that the culture of the organization had not been such as to encourage close cooperation between the various departments.

9. CARRY OUT A COST–BENEFIT ANALYSIS

A cost–benefit analysis is a standard business tool used to investigate the desirability of an activity or project by comparing the costs likely to be incurred with the benefits that will accrue using a financial basis. Training X costs $Y but over five years will provide a benefit of $3Y. Cost–benefit analysis is a decision-making tool that analyzes the viability of activities.

Whilst it may not always be easy to predict the exact financial benefit, cost–benefit analysis should always be undertaken. The results can provide powerful ammunition when it comes to selling the training and development strategy to the stakeholders in the organization.

The kind of negative comments from managers when consulted (or told!) about training and development are:

» "I can't release the person as we are too busy."
» "It costs too much money."
» "He or she might take up the training and development opportunity and then leave."
» "I can't spend the time in coaching and mentoring that will be needed."

The results from a properly conducted cost–benefit analysis may well provide an answer to such comments and show how the strategy will be a long-term investment rather than a short-term cost burden.

10. GAIN AGREEMENT FOR THE STRATEGY FROM ALL STAKEHOLDERS

To be successful, any organizational strategy needs agreement. Without agreement with the training and development strategy, those being trained and developed will not receive the support they deserve. The individual also needs to be in agreement with the strategy or else he or she may not put in the effort required. Volunteers are nearly always more motivated than conscripts.

Agreement should precede the training and development activities. Performance review meetings are an ideal opportunity for gaining agreement to the strategy and the training and development tactics between the individual and his or her manager or supervisor.

KEY LEARNING POINTS

In order to implement a training and development strategy:

1 it is necessary to understand the overall vision and goals of the organization;
2 the training and development strategy should be nested within the overall strategy of the organization;
3 the first step in developing a training and development strategy is to assess the current skills base of the organization;
4 it is then necessary to predict the skills that the organization will need in the future based on an analysis of the external environment;
5 how the gap between current and future skills will be bridged is an important component of the strategy;
6 success criteria for the strategy need to be put in place;
7 ensure that there are adequate resources for the strategy;
8 the strategy should avoid cultural conflict within parts of the organization;
9 a cost-benefit analysis should be carried out; and
10 agreement for the strategy needs to be gained from all stakeholders.

Frequently Asked Questions (FAQs)

Q1: What is the difference between strategy and tactics?

A: A training and development strategy can be defined as the direction and scope of the training and development opportunities developed and provided by the organization for its employees and other concerned partners: ideally which matches the training and development provided to both the needs of the organization and the individual in order to ensure that the organization can respond to changes in its external environment.

The training and development tactics are those shorter-term activities, programs, courses etc. that are used to bring the strategy to fruition.

You can read more about the definition of strategy in Chapter 2.

Q2: What are the components of a training and development strategy?

A: A training and development strategy comprises a number of components, all of which can be phrased as questions.

» What skills have our people at the moment?
» What are the future aims and direction of the organization?

» What skills will our people need to achieve the corporate aims?

The above form the basis for the overall strategy and a training needs analysis (TNA).

» From the TNA what training and development should be planned?
» Who will deliver the training and development?
» Who in the organization will receive the training and development?
» Are there stakeholders outside the organization who should receive training and development?

These components form the planning stage.

» How is the training and development to be implemented?

The implementation stage.

» How will the success of the training and development be monitored and evaluated?

This is the evaluation stage, which is likely to reveal new training needs. The process is cyclical, not linear, and is covered in Chapters 2 and 6 of this material.

Q3: What is meant by Continuous Professional Development?

A: Continuous Professional Development (CPD) is the requirement that many professions and jobs have for ongoing training and development to enable the individual to work with new technologies and systems. The standards and requirements are often laid down by professional bodies rather than the employing organization.
You can find out more about CPD in Chapter 3.

Q4: What role does ICT play in implementing a training and development strategy?

A: Information and Communication Technology (ICT) can allow greater flexibility in implementing a training and development strategy by simplifying issues of distance, location, time etc.
Chapter 4 covers the role of ICT in respect of training and development strategies.

Q5: What implications does globalization have for the implementation of training and development strategies?

A: Globalization and the concept of "thinking globally but acting locally" means that the training and development provided by a global organization, and hence the strategy from which the plans are derived, must consider issues of consistency and culture.

This area is covered in more detail in Chapter 5.

Q6: Why is it important that the training and development strategy is derived from and nested in the overall organization strategy?

A: The overall strategy of an organization represents the vision that the organization has for the future. All subordinate strategies, of which training and development is but one, should support the overall strategy. There should be a clearly identified link between the overall strategy and the training and development strategy so that those involved with the latter can see how it supports the overall strategy.

You can read more about this in Chapter 6.

Q7: Should a training and development strategy be concerned solely with improving the performance of current staff and equipping them with new skills for the future?

A: The improvement of performance and the acquisition of skills for the future are very important aspects of a training and development strategy. The strategy should, however, also address the role of training and development in:

» recruitment
» retention
» change management.

It is also worth considering whether training and development should be provided for major suppliers and customers.

These areas are covered in Chapter 6.

Q8: What is meant by a learning organization and core competencies?

A: A learning organization is one that displays skill in creating, acquiring, and transferring knowledge, and at modifying its behavior to reflect new knowledge and insights.

Competencies are a set of agreed standards that detail tasks a person should be able to undertake, the range of situations to which they apply, and the knowledge and understanding that relates to them. Core competencies are those skills that represent the fundamental expertise within the organization.

This subject is covered in Chapter 6 of this material.

Q9: What manner of success criteria should be in place as part of the training and development strategy?

A: The success criteria should be derived from a cost–benefit analysis and indicate what the organization expects from its investment. Success criteria should be written in the C-SMART format (Customer-centered, Specific, Measurable, Realistic, Agreed, and Time bound).

Once the success criteria are in place it becomes possible to evaluate the progress of the strategy in an objective manner. This allows any remedial action to be put into place quickly.

You can read more about this in Chapters 6 and 10.

Q10: Where can I find out about resources to assist in implementing a training and development strategy?

A: A list of books, journals and Web addresses will be found in Chapter 9. There are also other titles in the ExpressExec series that are dedicated to various facets of training and development.

Index

EXPRESSEXEC –
BUSINESS THINKING AT YOUR FINGERTIPS

ExpressExec is a 12-module resource with 10 titles in each module. Combined they form a complete resource of current business practice. Each title enables the reader to quickly understand the key concepts and models driving management thinking today.

Available from:
www.expressexec.com

Customer Service Department
John Wiley & Sons Ltd
Southern Cross Trading Estate
1 Oldlands Way, Bognor Regis
West Sussex, PO22 9SA
Tel: +44(0)1243 843 294
Fax: +44(0)1243 843 303
Email: cs-books@wiley.co.uk